Bonnie Fechters

WOMEN IN SCOTLAND
1900 ~ 1950

Sheila Livingstone

Foreword by Ruth Wishart

MOTHERWELL
SCOTTISH LIBRARY ASSOCIATION
1994

Contents

FOREWORD BY RUTH WISHART 3

NOR NAMED HER BONNIE NAME ~ introduction 4

BIRDS OF PASSAGE ~ women at work 6

A GUDE CAUSE ~ women and politics 16

WOMEN ~ The New Discovery ~ women at war 26

SWEATY SOCKS AND HERB WIVES ~ faith, hope and charity 35

ACKNOWLEDGEMENTS 46

FURTHER READING 46

TEACHERS NOTES ~ Ruth Currie 46

INDEX 47

To my mother
Margaret Peters
and all other women
who never had the chance
to fulfil their potential

Designed by GSB, Edinburgh.
Printed by Russell Print, Blantyre.

Scottish Library Association

Motherwell Business Centre,
Coursington Road, Motherwell.

© Sheila Livingstone 1994
ISBN 0 900649 89 5

With financial assistance from

THE SCOTTISH ARTS COUNCIL

FRONT COVER
'The Mill Girl',
by W. Strang
Cawder Golf Club,
Bishopbriggs

BACK COVER
'Service and Sacrifice',
Jane Haining.
Memorial windows in Strathbungo/
Queenspark Church, Glasgow.

Photography by Ken Willox.

INSIDE FRONT COVER
Illuminated address to
Agnes McDonald, Suffragist.
Women's Social & Political Union.
Edinburgh City Libraries.

INSIDE BACK COVER
A morale-boosting advertisement
to women farm workers, WW2.
Stirling Observer.

Introduction

Sheila Livingstone tells us that Scottish women have always suffered from something of an identity crisis. She does not lie. The thread which runs through this marvellously evocative record of Scotswomen's lives in the first fifty years of the 20th century is that of women struggling to find some expression for their natural talents within the appalling strictures which were imposed on their working and social lives. She underlines the paradox of men who thought it wholly unacceptable for their wives and daughters to have paid employment, yet had no qualms about the wives and daughters of other men cleaning their homes and preparing their meals. Many of the dilemmas women faced during these five decades were not, of course, peculiar to Scotland. The experiences of women working through two world wars to find poverty and unemployment at the other end was shared by women all over Britain. But it is rare to find such rich documentary material assembled which specifically reflects Scottish experience, and details personal Scottish histories. And some of the most delightful material comes from those personal reminiscences, much of it from oral history projects, some including folk songs recalling the female conditions of the day with characteristic wit. It is a commonplace to find women's lives and times completely deleted from historical accounts of Scotland. We seem subject to a strange brand of selective invisibility. Bonny Fechters does much to redress that infuriating imbalance.

Ruth Wishart. May 1994.

'Nor named her bonnie name'

MARION ANGUS

Scottish women have always had an identity crisis. Having been born into a patriarchal, mainly Presbyterian society, seen as inferior, constantly reminded that their place is in the home it is surprising that so many women, from 1900 onwards, showed that they were bonnie fechters.

Change is a slow uneven process. Some women, even today, will be leading lives similar to that of their mothers and grandmothers while others will be radically different. Not everyone's relations will have acted in the way then accepted as normal. Myths grow, sweeping statements are made until later generations believe them to be the whole truth and stereotypes are created.

The idea that no married women worked outside the home until the First World War or that women were inactive on the political scene can be questioned by studying the facts, reading contemporary sources and speaking to people who lived at that time.

The attitude of some men and often other women has played a part in deciding the status of women, denying them an individual identity. Their social position was determined by their husband's occupation and this attitude continued until recently. At the turn of the century Queen Victoria was Empress of India and reigned over an ever expanding empire. Britain, especially Clydeside, was known as 'the workshop of the world'. Yet, throughout Victoria's reign the majority of women became less their own person and more a chattel. *"Let women be*

From a programme for the Staff Social, March 1918. Dundee National Shell Factory. Dundee City Libraries

what God intended, a helpmate for man but with totally different duties and vocations," the Queen is quoted as saying.

At either end of the social spectrum they suffered. Those men who had risen in society by becoming the moguls of industry, to boost their own status, ensured that their mother, sister, wife or daughter was seen to do as little as possible. Those who were at the bottom end of the scale were driven from their family-based home industry to work in factories or as domestic servants to scrape a living. It may seem hypocritical by today's standards that men who treated their own female relatives as tender flowers to be shielded from the real world should employ other people's women to do their work.

It may appear that only the strong-minded, rebellious women managed to break the mould set by their upbringing. Others would try to make the best of the circumstances in which they found themselves and to better the situation of their neighbours. Only by researching the evidence and examining material from a variety of places and social backgrounds can any conclusions be drawn.

This book cannot hope to cover every aspect of women's lives from 1900 - 1950 but it will attempt to use primary and secondary sources and illustrations which, hopefully, are worthy of interpretation, to help the reader explore a variety of topics which can be followed up by further reading. Excluded are the worlds of the Arts, entertainment, science, the media and homelife which are only touched upon in relation to other topics.

Women rarely appear in dictionaries of biography or in history books. Even today it is difficult for teachers to find suitable material which is not stereotyped and the will to 'waste time' from more important aspects of history which examination candidates must learn about.

Although most published material is at an academic level and too detailed for the everyday reader, individual libraries and education resource services have produced local material which is interesting and accessible. This does not give an overall view without resort to a vast number of sources. I found an overwhelming and fascinating collection of evidence in oral history collections, local newspapers, academic books, archives and by speaking to people who have lived during the period covered. It is important not to apply today's standards when assessing the contribution which women have made to society. They must be judged against the background of their own time.

Women have been treated as a problem, their concerns trivialised, their experience demeaned. Prejudices in society have produced an image of women as being incomplete unless they are supported by a husband and have children to occupy their time. By expecting them to conform to a preconceived pattern their potential has been repressed and sacrifice has always been necessary for success unlike the scenario suggested by

'Marriages of the future would contain partners and all the stupid paraphernalia of rings, jewels, ornaments and cosmetics not being necessary to attract admiration, will vanish like a dream'

Tom Johnston. Forward 1912.

Eighty two years on, although much has been achieved many prejudices are still in force.

Bonnie Fechters ~ Women in Scotland 1900-1950

Birds of Passage

This was a description given by employers to their women workers. They were seen as passing the time between school and marriage by working, often in low paid jobs or in domestic service. The belief that every woman had a man to support her financially was the norm; a father until marriage then a husband. Women worked for 'pin' money. To accept otherwise required a redefining of roles and most men were too proud to allow their wives to work. They saw themselves as higher up the social ladder of respectability if their wives stayed at home. Nevertheless there were 270,000 women working in Scotland in 1911. While their working conditions were often poor they were much the same as those of men. The majority of workers toiled for hours which today seem excessive, had few rights and could be easily dismissed without recourse to a tribunal. There were few 'lasses o' pairts' being sent off to university from humble beginnings, and so many clever women had no chance of ever realising their potential.

Widows were eagerly sought after by employers. They were considered reliable and honest because they needed to work in order to support their family. In the 1930's a widows pension was introduced to help alleviate this problem. In the textile trade some women worked as outworkers finishing garments in their own homes for a pitiful wage. A Royal Commission was set up to investigate the situation but no amount of legislation or factory acts could guarantee improvement. There were never enough inspectors to go round and many women were afraid to complain in case they lost their job.

Edinburgh was home to the main national institutions and business headquarters while Glasgow had a high level of skilled artisans. These different circumstances resulted in both cities being male dominated.

Washerwomen, c1900. Strathkelvin District Libraries

Textile towns tended however to employ a high percentage of women, but never as foremen or managers. Brechin, Forfar and the Border towns provided low paid work in the mills. Dundee was known as the 'She' Town: there were 3 women to every 2 men in the age group 20 - 49 in 1900. Unlike other areas 24% of Dundee's married women worked, many in the jute industry. Dundee was also a town of one-parent families long before the term was invented and many men relied on the wages of their mothers or sisters. Comparable figures were Glasgow 6% and Edinburgh 5% .

By the 1950's one third of the Scottish workforce was female. The economic character of each area of Scotland differed. On leaving school at fourteen most girls had little option but to go into whichever industries were prominent where they lived. Greenock had canvas weaving, sugar refineries and confectioners, Dundee jute, Dumfermline linen and the Borders woollens. In the Highlands it was crofting which prevailed. In town and country alike domestic service was the most common occupation for women followed by work in the mill or factory.

Your mother or sister who worked there before you put in a word with the foreman and you were taken on. Shop work and waitressing were other options. There was plenty of work at the beginning of the century but in 1910 unemployment spread and there was general unrest. This was short lived because of the onset of WW1 in August 1914. After the war there was recession and massive unemployment in the 1920's and 1930's alleviated only by the build up to WW2.

Girls who had an education could become teachers, missionaries, nurses and occasionally doctors or scientists. A growing number of middle-class girls had managed to defy the strict code of Victorian behaviour and map out a career for themselves. However, even in teaching and nursing which employed a high proportion of women they were often given the low status jobs or temporary appointments. The more traditional roles of nannies or governesses were still to the fore. Those who lived in the country or near the sea could work on the land or help with the fishing. In the Highlands and Islands and in the really rural areas women were still equal partners as they had been elsewhere in the days of handloom weaving.

Bonnie Fechters ~ Women in Scotland 1900-1950

DOMESTIC SERVICE

In St. Andrews, 24% and in Broughty Ferry, 20% of working women were employed in domestic service compared to 16% in Edinburgh. The work meant long hours for little money. Some employers only paid wages every six months. The usual pattern was to start as a kitchen or general maid and live in. Some employers were good to their staff but others were mean. One report mentions one prune each for breakfast and three eggs amongst six servants. Staffs could be as small as one or more than thirty five, in a large establishment. In the latter there could be five servants sleeping in one room leaving little chance of privacy.

Servants were often employed through agencies run by women such as Miss Glass, in Glasgow. Others were found by placing an advertisement in the newspaper and for butlers and lady's maids in periodicals such as *The Lady*. Nannies tended to come by personal recommendation from the families in which they were employed.

Sometimes there were as many as eight staff employed to look after one person with all the ritual of serving meals in silver covered tureens in the dining room at every meal. The system was hierarchical with each department in a large mansion keeping within its own boundaries and with senior staff waited upon by the lower staff. Everybody 'knew their place'. In a very large establishment there might also be a first and second coachman or chauffeur, a groom, a lady's maid and a nanny.

The last two positions considered themselves a step above the rest and may have had their own quarters perhaps with a sitting-room as well as a bedroom. They had the chance to travel with the family and might also have a personal maid of their own.

One lady's maid describes being sent to Garrards, the Royal jeweller in London, to learn how to look after and clean her mistress's jewellery.

Another well known problem of domestic service was sexual harassment. In 1910 a National Vigilance Committee was set up to protect Highland girls who came to work in the cities. Members met girls arriving on long-distance trains, and those coming off the boat-trains from Ireland. There were hostels at which the girls could stay until they found a position with a family.

Housemaid, 1903. J. Sanderson

Domestic service was seen by the establishment as a way forward in the reformation of girls from the Industrial Schools which existed to deal with wrongdoers too young to go to prison. The Onward and Upward Association was an attempt for example by Ishbel, Countess of Aberdeen to help improve the chances of girls in her service by giving them an education. This organisation spread until there were branches in Canada and Ireland.

A DAY IN A SCOTTISH HOME

'My mother took me to Glasgow to register with an agency when I was fifteen and I started in the west end of Glasgow in a big mansion. I got £18.00 a year plus keep. I was there for six months then I went as 4th housemaid to Helensburgh and I got £28.00 per year. We got up at 6am and cleaned the public rooms. You musn't be seen. If anyone came you picked up your huckaback which protected the carpet and all your cleaning things and you disappeared. I used to joke 'do they think it's the fairies that do the work.'

At 8.30 you went to your room to change into a clean white apron and cap, roll down your sleeves and line up with the other servants. The housekeeper went first, the cook, the lady's maid then us, then the kitchen maids, the scullery maid, the hallboy, 2nd footman, 1st footman, the chauffeur, 2nd chauffeur and the butler. You had an early breakfast then when the family were breakfasting you did the bedrooms. I polished the landings on my hands and knees. There were no Hoovers then. I had 2 hours off after lunch.

At 4 o'clock it was afternoon tea. The 4th maid, me, had to prepare the servants' tea, then the butler had his in the pug's parlour served by the hall-boy, who was training to be a footman. The kitchen staff made the tea and you knocked when you entered the kitchen to collect it. Then dinner was prepared and served and after dinner you were free but you usually fell into bed.'

Stirling Women's Oral History Project 1988.

Being a lady's maid was a more prestigious position. This is an account of the work of one woman whose mistress was a duchess. The maid rose at about 6am and had her own breakfast. She then checked that her mistress's clothes were laid out. Many ladies had functions to attend or 'at homes' to conduct and the correct items, including jewellery, would have been discussed the night before. She wakened her mistress around 7am having run her bath.

She looked after her mistress's clothes in the morning, cleaning and pressing them, but had the afternoon off. She then laid out evening clothes, as her mistress would change for dinner even if she were staying at home. She did not wear a uniform but a black dress and she had staff to look after her rooms. Her meals were served in her sitting-room and she rarely mixed with the general staff. She travelled with the family to London and abroad and went with them on visits to other aristocratic homes.

Some girls from orphanages were sent to the colonies as servants.

Lenzie Girls for Canada.

One of the first passenger ships to leave the Clyde this year for Canada was the Canadian Pacific Duchess of York which sailed from the Tail of the Bank on Saturday 8th August. Included in the emigrant list was a party of 28 girls who for the past 10 weeks have been taking a course of training in household work at the Ministry of Labour Hostel at Millersneuk. Guaranteed situations, mostly in Ontario, have been secured for these girls. Their wages in the beginning of their service will not be less than £4.00 per month.

Kirkintilloch Herald. August 1930.

Not all domestic service was live in. Many women were daily cleaners at factories, schools and offices. Laundresses often worked 16 to 17 hours per day. It was a hard and tiring job. Other women cooked and served in institutions and hospitals where they also worked long hours. Day servants were employed from 8am to 6pm. Washerwomen worked 4 or 6 hours for 2/6 plus 1/- for ironing.

DECLINE OF DOMESTIC SERVICE

After WW1 the number of women willing to undertake the strict discipline of 'no male callers', half-day off per week and one day off per month fell. In rural areas in particular the restricted social life and the inconvenience of living out in the country were felt by women attracted to the shorter hours and more money available in the towns.

FACTORIES AND MILLS

worked from 6am-6pm but in 1910 the mills had a later start of 8am with 1 hour for dinner from 12 - 1pm. There were no tea breaks but metal cans were carried and hot water provided to make tea. If you were late for work your money was 'docked" and you lost wages. Girls and women used to run like mad to get under the door before it closed.

1. Vindanda Laundry, Kirkintilloch. c1910.
(Strathkelvin District Libraries).

2. Weaving shed, Dens, Dundee. c1910.
(University of Dundee Archives).

3. Women waiting to be searched, ICI factory, Stevenson, Ayrshire. c1910.
(Cunninghame District Libraries).

Mary Brooksbank [1897-1980]:

was a mill girl in Dundee though she was born in Aberdeen in 1897. As soon as she was 14 her mother took her to see the foreman who found her 'a richt wee smerter'. It was the morning after the sinking of the Titanic. She worked 12 hour shifts from 6am to 6pm. for 7/6 per week. The work was hard but Mary enjoyed making up wee rhymes about the people she saw around her, the conditions under which they worked and the uppishness of those in charge so full of their own importance.

Mary read widely about politics and listened to street speakers who drew crowds seeking entertainment; there was no radio or television in those days. Brought up as a Catholic she renounced her faith and became a Communist because she thought that they could change the world and wipe out poverty. Arrested several times at demonstrations she was imprisoned at Perth in 1919 on Armistice Day for breach of the peace. Communists were anti-war considering it an imperialist con trick. On her release she formed the Working Women's Guild which attracted 300 members. They sent deputations to the Town Council and to Maryfield, the poor relief hospital, on behalf of the aged and poor inmates. They held meetings outside the Poorhouse and members began to chair meetings and speak in public on behalf of working women.

Mary challenged society's view of women. She led the

Bonnie Fechters ~ Women in Scotland 1900-1950

'It was no job for a pensioner' was how one woman described her work. She was jumping about all day amidst the clackety clack of the looms. Like many in the mill she was paid on piecework. If the machine broke down she lost wages. As a fully fledged weaver she could earn 24/- per week for three webs which were 84ft. each. This was in a sailmakers. Weavers in Dundee considered themselves a cut above the other mill girls and always wore a hat.

Some jobs involved heavy lifting. One of these was in a sugar refinery where barrels of syrup had to be rolled along and sacks of sugar carried by women workers on their backs. In a confectionery factory the women carried 2 cwt sacks of icing sugar and ran with them to the dry store. The fondant icing which was made there was sticky yet there were no washing facilities. It was possible to keep working after marriage but the majority did not stay on. Most women started a family soon after they married.

To relieve the boredom of routine work singing by the women all day long is mentioned in many testimonies and one union leader during a fishing net work strike at Kilbirnie in Ayrshire in 1913 suggested that the women should

OCCUPATION OF WOMEN IN GLASGOW, 1931 AND 1951, AND SCOTLAND 1951

Occupation order	Number in Glasgow 1931	Number in Glasgow 1951	Percentage of all occupied women 1951 Glasgow	Percentage of all occupied women 1951 Scotland
Fishermen	–	–	–	–
Agricultural, horticultural and forestry occupations	308	157	.09	2.13
Mining and quarrying occupations	12	2	.00	.01
Workers in the treatment of non-metalliferous mining products (other than coal)	651	399	.23	.19
Coal, gas and coke makers, workers in chemical and allied trades	278	168	.10	.36
Workers in metal manufacture, engineering and allied trades	1,704	2,935	1.72	1.54
Textile workers	9,128	6,220	3.66	8.22
Tanners etc., leather goods makers, fur dressers	1,112	1,147	.67	.25
Makers of textile goods and articles of dress (not boots and shoes)	16,698	17,609	10.35	5.38
Makers of foods, drinks and tobacco	5,307	4,758	2.80	2.40
Workers in wood, cane and cork	412	567	.33	.06
Makers of and workers in paper and paperboard, bookbinders, printers	5,000	4,282	2.52	1.69
Makers of products not elsewhere specified	1,327	781	.46	.47
Workers in building and contracting	2	56	.03	.07
Painters and decorators	1,476	1,034	.61	.45
Administrators, directors and managers	489	634	.37	.48
Persons employed in transport and communication	4,619	5,546	3.26	2.35
Commercial, finance and insurance occupations	28,687	25,201	14.81	14.04
Professional and technical occupations	10,775	13,029	7.66	9.32
Persons employed in defence service	28	241	.14	.17
Persons professionally engaged in entertainments and sport	435	419	.25	.16
Persons engaged in personal service	38,926	30,240	17.78	22.30
Clerks, typists etc.	24,311	38,058	22.37	20.09
Warehousewomen, store keepers, packers bottlers	6,379	6,524	3.83	2.72
Stationary engine drivers, crane drivers, etc., stokers etc.	11	62	.04	.07
Workers in unskilled occupations	4,912	8,776	5.16	4.66
Other and undefined workers	902	1,306	.77	.41
Total gainfully occupied	163,889	170,151	100.00	100.00

3rd Statistical Account of Scotland: Glasgow 1958.

Railway Women's Guild who supported her in 1927, when she was again in prison for heckling, by sending her meals. Eventually she was expelled from the Communist Party for criticising Stalin.

Her poems and songs live on, the best known being an adaptation of a popular folksong, Oh Dear Me, about life in the mill.

OH DEAR ME
Oh, dear me, the mill's gaen fest,
The puir wee shifters canna get a rest,
Shiftin bobbins, coorse and fine,
They fairly mak' ye work for your ten and nine
Oh, dear me, I wish the day was done,
Runnin' up and doon the pass is no nae fun;
Shiftin' piecin', spinnin' warp, weft and twine,
Tae feed and cled my bairnie affen ten and nine.
Oh, dear me, the world's ill divided,
Them that works the hardest are aye wi' least provided,
But I maun bide contented, dark days or fine,
But there's no much pleasure livin' affen ten and nine.
[ten and nine was then the wage per week.]

She also describes the life and ambitions of another girl whose father was killed during WW1 and whose friend's fiance was killed while fighting with the International Brigade during the Spanish Civil War. Many Scots men and women joined the International Brigade and fought in the Spanish Civil War. The Battle of Tereul took place in 1937 and was an anti-fascist victory.

A DUNDEE LASSIE
I'm a Dundee lassie, you can see,
You'll aye find me cheerful
Nae matter whar I be;
Tho' at times I feel doonhearted, sad or ill.
I'm a spinner intae Baxter's Mill.
My mither dee'd when I was young.
My father fell in France.
I'd liked tae been a teacher,
But I never got the chance.
I'll soon be getting married
Tae a lad ca'd Tammy Hill.
He's an iler intae Halley's Mill
I'm chumming wi' a lassie,
They ca' her Teenie Bain.
She says she'll never mairry.
Her lad got kilt in Spain:
I aften hear her speak aboot
A place they ca' Tereul.
She's a winder intae Craigie Mill.
From Sidlaw Breezes - Mary Brooksbank- David Winter-Dundee.

Bonnie Fechters ~ Women in Scotland 1900-1950

form a choir. The Newhaven Fishwives did and performed at many functions.

Some factories, such as Singer Sewing Machines at Clydebank were patriarchal and provided well for their workers. From the 1930's onwards there were sports grounds and a hall for numerous activities. There was a band and choirs as well as sewing and embroidery classes and clubs covering every interest.

Outings were always arranged in the workers' own time. At one coalmine dancing until 10 o'clock at the pithead after work was a popular way of passing an evening.

LEGISLATION

The Factory Acts were a double-edged sword enabling the trade unions to have certain occupations classed as 'unsuitable' for women. In the guise of protecting women workers male trade unionists really were reacting to what they saw as a threat to men's monopoly of these jobs. Rather than tackle the real problems faced by women, such as poverty, the need for adequate childcare and better health care they effectively banned women from certain workplaces. Married women whether they had children or not

1. Callaghan's Fruiterer & Florist, Clydebank.
Clydebank District Libraries

2. Greenlees & Sons, shoeshop, Glasgow.
c1930
Catherine Millar.

Margaret Peters (left) [1903-1988]:

worked in Birrell's the confectioners. She became manageress of the shop in Union Street, Glasgow in 1926.

'We had to wear black dresses at all times and on a Saturday at 4.00pm changed into black lace evening dresses or long black skirts and white lace blouses which we had to supply ourselves. In those days every box of chocolates was made up by hand from the customer's own selection. We often had to deliver these to the theatres. We worked from 8am - 6pm Monday to Friday with a half day on a Tuesday and did not close on Saturday night until 11.00pm. On Christmas Eve we worked until midnight'.
Personal interview, Abbeyfield, Lenzie 1986.

Mrs Mackie [1900-]:

worked in McCulloch and Young's Department Store in Stirling in the 1930's. She was lucky to get a job during the recession.

'There was no dole money in those days. I worked in the china department. I had a great deal of dusting to do. If you got a big order it had to be packed in a box carefully, with straw. I worked from 9am to 6.30pm every day and had a halfday on a Wednesday. I got 7/- a week but by the time I got married in 1933 I had 17/6.'

She was asked to go back to help out during WW2 and was put in charge of the china department.

From: Five Bob a Week-Stirling Women's Work 1900-1950, edited by Joyce Stevenson, 1988.

Bonnie Fechters ~ Women in Scotland 1900-1950

Sweated Workers in Glasgow

STRIKE OF WAITRESSES AT KERR'S CAFES

Citizens of Glasgow, your attention is drawn to the conditions which prevail at above establishments:

Waitresses and Kitchen Staff are receiving the following Wages and Conditions:—

12/- per week for 12 hours per day

1/-	deducted if girl breaks a plate
9d	„ „ „ cup
6d	„ „ „ saucer
2/-	„ „ „ wineglass
3d	„ for being late in morning

'The Girls decided to join the Union, with the result that the Shop Steward was dismissed, which is quite evidently an attempt to undermine the Girls' Union.

Previous to joining the Union, the minimum wage of restaurant workers was 10/- per week, and they had to purchase uniform from the firm

We are asking the public to

SUPPORT THE GIRLS

Broadsheet stating the grievances of Kerr's waitresses, who went on strike in January 1920.

Pettigrew and Stephens 'A corner of the tea room' in 1909.

were often denied work in case men might be tempted to live off their wives' earnings.

It was the same for women who had taken up employment during WW1. Ideas of their worth in industry changed when recession came between the wars and it was back to the status quo. Women teachers were obliged to resign on marriage until the mid 1940's as was sometimes the case in local government and the Civil Service until the mid 1960's After WW2 there were better and more varied opportunities for the employment of women.

RETAIL TRADE

The retail and warehouse trades, catering and hotel work demanded long hours and were sore on the feet. In 1901 Margaret Irwin of the Scottish Council For Women's Trade campaigned against shop assistants having to work a 14-16 hour day. Many shops stayed open on weekdays till midnight. Shop assistants made up a large proportion of women workers. Most commodities were sold loose. Sugar had to be bagged, butter and cheese cut and bacon sliced.

CATERING

Waitresses were in demand as tearooms expanded. Many were well run, the City Bakeries having a profit sharing scheme, but others paid the minimum wage which in 1920 was 10/- minus a charge for the uniform and a fine for every plate or cup which got broken. Staff were expected to stay late if there was a function, for no extra pay. Some waitresses joined the National Federation of Women Workers.

Kate Cranston [1849 -1934]

broke with tradition by becoming a business woman. Her aunt, Elizabeth Dalgleish was a hotelier in equal partnership with her husband, Robert. He believed in educating women and gave his daughter Mary a temperance hotel as a wedding present. He offered to finance Kate enabling her to open her first tearoom in 1878. In 1892 she married John Cochrane but in true Scottish tradition continued to trade under her own name. Her brother Stuart was also a restaurateur. Men patronised tearooms and coffee shops at this time rather than take their morning break at their desk.

She caused a sensation when she chose Charles Rennie Mackintosh to carry out the interior design for her tearooms, from the furnishings down to the teaspoons, making the Willow Tearoom the most talked about and fashionable one in the kingdom. Kate's husband died in 1917 and she retired from public life. She sold the house which Mackintosh had designed for them and moved into the North British Station Hotel opposite George Square in Glasgow. She dressed in black until her own death in 1934.

She had trained and encouraged many women to follow her lead. Her manageresses Miss Rose Rombach and Miss Margaret Buick went on to establish their own empires. She was a model employer with a large staff. She gave preference to girls from orphanages and single-parent homes when she appointed waitresses and took out insurance to cover their medical expenses. She was a disciplinarian who set high standards. The waitresses worked long hours 8am -8pm for 4/- plus 3 good meals per day. There were table waitresses, cashiers, cooks, potato maids, vegetable maids, stew maids and pudding maids. Nails were inspected every day and clean and neat hosiery and petticoats were to be worn.

Bonnie Fechters ~ Women in Scotland 1900-1950

BUSINESS WOMEN

It was in the retail sector that many women owned their own businesses. Ladies outfitters, drapery, fancy goods, newsagents, bakers, grocers and fish shops were popular. The premises were often rented but the business was owned.

Other women did work in a man's world. After the death of a husband or father with whom they had worked closely the woman would take charge of the office and staff, the yard or store, assisted by chargehands or foremen, and having proved knowledgeable would gain respect in her own right.

Ethel and Willie Baxter
Baxter's of Speyside

Maggie McIver [1879-1958]:

She started as a ragwoman and rose to fame and fortune as Queen of the Barras. The Barras are Glasgow's open market, a large array of stalls. When Maggie began she had three spare barrows which she hired out. By 1926 she had established a covered market in Moncur Street and by 1928 permanent stalls were available. Many of the stallholders were women. Every year she gave a Christmas meal, drink and dance to her staff. One year the usual hall was booked up so she built the famous Barrowland Ballroom above the market. When she died in 1958 she was a wealthy woman.

Ethel Baxter [1883 - 1963]:

was born on a farm at Roseisle in Morayshire and trained at Aberdeen Royal Infirmary as a nurse. She specialised in midwifery and then took up private nursing. She met her future husband, Willie Baxter, as a patient, and married into the successful Fochabers grocery firm which bought only local produce and had become famous for its jams, which her mother-in-law, Margaret Baxter had perfected in 1868. Ethel had an astute business mind and saw that the shop would not support all the family. She persuaded Willie to borrow money and set up a factory on the opposite bank of the Spey where they also specialised in jam and marmalade making. She was an equal partner from the start and worked at the factory where she learned about the maintenance of the machinery as well as the production side. Willie was the salesman and toured the country.

After WW1 she persuaded him to take samples to the very top and he approached the grocery buyer of Harrods in London who was impressed by the quality of the goods and placed an order. Soon the Baxters were selling to exclusive shops in New York, Chicago and Johannesburg.

Ethel worked a twelve hour day as well as running her home and looking after her two sons with the help of a nanny. In 1929 she invented Royal Game soup, beetroot in vinegar and tinned haggis. As the selection grew so did the demand and they spread the net wider for suppliers of good wholesome ingredients.

No matter how busy she was she also worked for charity raising funds for the many causes which she supported including the local Episcopalian Church. In 1952 her son Gordon, who is now the chairman, married an art teacher, Ena, who followed her mother-in-law's example and found that her speciality was in making interesting soups, especially Cock-a-leekie and Lobster Bisque. To keep up the tradition her son Andrew's wife, Amanda, specialises in developing sauces. Baxters of Speyside sell to hotels and stores world-wide and even make an exclusive soup which is delivered every August to the Queen at Balmoral. Ethel died in 1963 and is buried overlooking the sea. She would be delighted to know that her granddaughter,

Audrey, now the Company's Managing Director, has her rightful place on the Board beside her brothers. Ethel's intuition and hard work helped to build a firm whose visitor centre is a major attraction for tourists, and the Company gives employment to many, especially women, in the North East.

Elizabeth Dunlop (above) [1920-]:

'My father was a manufacturer's agent and when he died suddenly in December 1946 I decided to continue in business for a few months, really to wind things up. To begin with I knew absolutely nothing about the business as I had been an accountant officer in the Air Force.

Bonnie Fechters ~ Women in Scotland 1900-1950

FARMWORK

The contribution of women to farmwork has been largely ignored, even estate records fail to record the lives of the women who worked on them even although some became factors on the death of their husbands. Most were born into this work and from childhood stooked sheaves, carried peat and learned how to milk a cow. Many married farmers and continued working all their lives.

Women claimed as their own the 'egg' money. Many had a run with loyal customers to whom they supplied eggs, hens and chickens. This money was often spent not on themselves but went to improve their surroundings, paying for installing electricity, bathrooms, Aga cookers and even towards farming equipment but mostly only on their on their say-so. One woman saved up for new teeth then decided to buy a sewing machine instead.

In the Hebrides, Orkney and Shetland women were often involved in the gathering and spreading of seaweed and in burning the kelp. This was common also in Galloway. Other work included digging for bait and gathering whelks for which they were paid 5/- per bushel. By the 1950's many island women who had gone off to the mainland to school preferred to find work away from home, especially in the cities, and populations declined. For those who remained life continued much as before, only from the 1960's did roles begin to change.

There were few lady agents and manufacturers were just beginning to come to life after the restrictions of the war years. Commercial travelling was very much a man's world. The firms which my father had worked with did not want a lady agent as they had never had one but agreed to keep me on for a trial period. I was so anxious to succeed and make ends meet that I did not realise that the testing time had elapsed and eventually I retired 40 years later in 1986.
My job was to sell the manufacturers' products to the wholesale drapery warehousemen of whom there were a great many in Glasgow, Aberdeen and Edinburgh. They in turn sold to the retail drapers. I don't know when I began to enjoy the job and relish the challenge of securing large orders and ensuring them delivered correctly and on time. It was not an easy job with hard work and few holidays. There was no security but it was wonderfully interesting. In 1969 I was appointed as the first lady president of the Scottish Association of Manufacturers' Agents'.
Eastwood District Libraries

Agnes Tod [1895-1988]:

lived at Corsehope Farm in Midlothian. Her father was a grieve and they always had plenty to eat. Many girls went off to domestic service and did not do field work but she helped her father and one brother who was still at home.

'It was usually at harvest times or potato lifting and clipping, that sort o' thing. I didn't shear the sheep myself. I just rolled up the wool. And I liked that job you had nice soft hands when you were finished. At harvest time I worked from daylight till dark if it was dry. I've seen us working by moonlight to get it done. When I first started I was fourteen and I got 3/6 per week. In 1919 I got 30/- ,after that I got married and I didnae need any wages.'
Hard Work Ye Ken, Four Midlothian Women Farmworkers - edited by Ian MacDougall, Canongate, 1994.

Not everyone who was connected with work on the land was brought up on a farm.

HOGGIE'S ANGELS ~ Belle Lindsay [1895-]:

From 1910 she worked around the Dalkeith area for Bobby Hogg, a potato merchant. This was a job which needed stamina as it was backbreaking and involved heavy lifting. At fifteen she got up at 5am and walked to the yard to start at 6am

'I wasnae fed tae cairry thur big bags o' tatties.'

They were expected to humph a hundredweight of potatoes on their backs up stairs to an attic.

'Hingin' on tae the bannister wi' yin hand and haudin the bag wi' the other an' yer knees knockin'

is how she describes it. There were eight or nine girls employed in this task and they were called Hoggie's Angels by the locals.
Hard Work Ye Ken, Four Midlothian Women Farmworkers - edited by Ian MacDougall, Canongate, 1994.

---

1. Women workers wearing 'uglies', Lothian. c1943.
Scotsman Publications

2. Milkmaids, Garthamlock Farm, Glasgow
Catherine Barries.

3. Gathering the shaws, Mid-Calder, 1950's.
National Museum of Scotland

4. Going to 'lift' peats. c1930.
Third Eye Centre.

Bonnie Fechters ~ Women in Scotland 1900-1950

FISHING

was also a hard life but here at least the women worked as equal partners with the men. The women of the North East were considered to be the most liberated in Scotland. They controlled their own money and the right to sell fish from a creel was passed down through the female line. Many continued to be fishwives even when they were married to men who worked at another trade. These women often owned property and were economically independent.

In Auchmithie, near Arbroath the women would launch the boat and when the men returned they carried them on their backs to the shore. It was the women who mended nets and gutted fish. *'We turned our hand to whatever needed to be done. We were partners.'*

The men could be away at sea for some time and the women looked after the family and supported each other in a close knit community which sometimes could feel claustrophobic. Everybody knew everyone else's business.

Some girls and women followed the fishing fleet down to Great Yarmouth where the herring boats would dock. They worked together as a crew of three. Two to gut and one to pack, working an eighteen hour day from 6am to 1am. They tied their fingers with thread to try to protect them against cuts and hacks which stung from the salt. There was no cover above them and they either suffered sunburn, freezing cold or soakings.

During WW2 fishgutters were paid off because German action prevented the boats from going to sea. In the 1950's fish processing factories were opened where fish was canned or made into paste. Quick freeze methods were also used to freeze the fresh catch. Many women were employed at Lossiemouth and Wick factories in this type of work.

COALMINING

In contrast in 1910 girls were still working as surface workers in the coalmines.

1. Mrs Swanson, a Thurso fishwife.
2. Elizabeth Sutherland, 'Labour Liz'
3. Herring workers.
4. Quick freeze factory.
From 'Over the Ord' by Herbert Sinclair.

5. Shettleston Colliery surface workers, mostly young girls removing stones from coal passing along a conveyor belt. c1910.
From 'Shettleston Past and Present', by Thomas Waugh.

6. Air taxi girl, Winifred Drinkwater standing beside her air taxi at St. Andrews. 1934.
East Fife Courier.

7. Cartoon depicting policewomen from Dundee City Libraries Photographic Collection

Bonnie Fechters ~ Women in Scotland 1900-1950

FLYERS AND FEATHER BOAS

There were many unusual and unexpected occupations: from folding newspapers by hand and furling feather boas to piloting an air taxi in 1934. A complaint was lodged in Stirling in 1923 that women should not be allowed to sweep the streets. In Dundee in 1918 a police sister was appointed to deal with wayward girls and women and from then on the number of women in the force grew, much to the amusement of the populace as this cartoon shows. It was 1945 before policewomen were permanently appointed in Fife, having served as auxiliaries during WW2. Out of 274 police in Dunbartonshire in 1955 only 11 were women and it was 1960 before such an appointment was made in Airdrie.

Dressmakers, tailoresses and hairdressers were amongst those who had to pay for their training. This limited entry to those whose families could afford the fees.

It was the 1919 Sex Disqualification [Removal] Act which allowed women to serve on juries, become solicitors and enter the professions. Printing actually forced women out while in journalism, laboratory work, the Civil Service, librarianship and many other professions openings occurred. Although in many jobs the workforce was mainly female, even in teaching, those at the top were still, usually, male.

In so many interviews regret is expressed about restrictions of choice. Many record that the headteacher asked that girls be allowed to 'stay on' but that the money just wasn't there. Hairdressers wanted to be pharmacists, shop girls to play the piano, sing with a band, paint pictures but these were dreams, as most of them had to stick to work which brought in a regular wage. Many wanted to be teachers or nurses but went to work in an office to let a brother have his chance of moving up the social ladder. They were like caged birds more than birds of passage.

Mrs Quentin:

was from Bellshill in Lanarkshire and worked at a pit.

'I thought I wasn't getting a big enough pay and I went to the gaffer and got a job lamp cleaning. I worked three shifts 6am to 4pm; backshift 2pm to 10.30pm and night shift 9pm to 7am. I was there till all the lamps were given out. When we finished at night, especially in the winter, one of the men would bring out his accordion and we would dance from 7 o'clock till 10 o'clock at the corner of the buildings.'

Janetta Bowie (above) [1907-]:

always wanted to be a teacher. She was dux of Greenock High School in 1925, and winner of the Sir Godfrey Collins Prize for English. Although her father died when she was fifteen her mother decided to allow her to carry on with her education. She attended Glasgow University and worked every holiday to help with expenses. In 1928 she graduated M.A., having abandoned the 2nd half of the English [Honours] Course because of her mother's illness. There were many women in her year who, like herself, went to Jordanhill College of Education to become teachers, although at that time at the end of the 1920's, students outnumbered jobs two to one. By the time she was 21 she had achieved her ambition and was appointed to Jean Street School, Port Glasgow. Later she took the course in Infant School Methods, as that qualification was the only opening for promotion.

She recorded her memories of her teaching days in several successful books, the first being *Penny Buff*.

'I remember the men at university being well dressed in their blazers, collar and ties, many wearing hats. The most alarming experience that I remember was seeing droves of working men converge on the University during the General Strike of 1926 because they were angry with the male students who were driving tramcars to keep the service going.'

Janetta never married because her career meant so much to her and in those days teachers were forced to resign on marriage.

Personal interview. Greenock, 1993.

Bonnie Fechters ~ Women in Scotland 1900-1950

A Gude Cause

I'd love to change the world but I have to cook the tea.

For the majority of women in the early part of the 20th century being considered 'respectable' was very important. This did not apply only to the middle class; the bulk of working class women were no exception. If there was any chance of climbing the social ladder, even if it meant moving house from one side of a railway line to the 'better' side, most women wanted to be in a position to take it. A factor's line was needed to get another house. This was a sort of reference recommending you as good tenants who paid rent on time.

Divorce was frowned on and rarely spoken about or even considered as the stigma was so great. With the exception of some women among the upper classes wives stayed married Not only was the legal process costly, many divorced women would have ended up without a roof over their heads. You made your bed and lay in it. Only 44 legal separations took place in 1900 and a mere 7 in 1912. It was not until 1969 that the Divorce Reform Act simplified the procedure and permitted divorce without the need for specific grounds such as adultery or mental cruelty. Legal aid was also made available and a fifty-fifty split of all assets introduced.

The burden of making ends meet, ensuring that the children were clothed and fed, dealing with factors, organising repairs to the home, all these responsibilities fell upon women. In their own right they were coping with social and political actions but they were unaware of this fact. A woman had a higher status as wife of someone than as a person and often sunk her own identity in that of her family. She took pride in the occupations of her husband and children, living life at second hand through them.

"I say Bill, I doubt we've got into no man's land."
Dundee City Libraries.

Those who did not marry were often pitied and expected to be at the beck and call of their parents or married siblings. Many had little belief in their own capabilities. Working class women only slowly realised that their contribution to the community was valuable. They simply accepted the opinions of their husbands and made no attempt to think for themselves. On the whole the upper and middle classes had more confidence albeit in a limited way, and could be found as presidents and chairwomen of many voluntary societies and organisations.

This does not mean that women were not politically active. The definition of politics is male orientated however and the issues with which women are often identified are treated as domestic or trivial rather than as offering possible solutions to what are male imposed problems. Flexible hours, nurseries and creches, maternity leave and job sharing are treated as diluting the norm. Instead of moving forward both trade unions and employers tended to be set in their ways through fear of change or its results.

Women are more likely to campaign for a cause in which they passionately believe, to settle a conflict, to redress an injustice, to right what they see as a wrong rather than consider joining a specific political party. Nevertheless, Scottish women, especially in areas such as Dundee and Glasgow, were more involved in political action than their English counterparts and many middle and upper-class women understood and were appalled at the plight of the working-class.

Women began to form a network, through involvement in a variety of national organisations, which is much wider than is generally considered. Many of the women mentioned in this book appear in more than one context. Women of differing political views, from a variety of professions, as members of trade unions and from all classes knew each other through involvement in the suffrage movement, rent strikes, industrial action, peace movements, temperance campaigns, voluntary social work and hunger marches. As the century advanced they were taking part in such activities in ever-increasing numbers.

Participation in these movements and attending meetings throughout Scotland, helping to organise, publicise and speak in the cause of suffrage and taking the campaign to towns, villages and workplaces where men and women could listen to their arguments and heckle them gave many women the confidence to present themselves as candidates for political office. This resumé barely scratches the surface of the political activity in which women took part. It was not, as is often suggested, only stairhead fights in which women were involved but action to address genuine causes and attempts to change attitudes towards women and their concerns.

formed. In 1914 its members demonstrated in London on behalf of women's right to vote but Herbert Asquith, the Prime Minister, refused to grant them an audience although they did speak with the Scottish Members of Parliament. There were 100 men on the platform at another protest meeting in London which impressed the English suffragists and showed them that the matter was being taken seriously in Scotland.

'The campaign for the right to vote was part of a wider struggle of women's rights to education, to economic independence and to work'

Eleanor Gordon in People and Society in Scotland,

Not all men took it seriously though and some local government councillors thought it a 'laughing matter'. Suffragists became the butt of jokes and cartoons.

In 1908 a suffragist wrote to complain about her rough treatment in Kirkintilloch. In the following week's *Kirkintilloch Herald* this poem appeared.

*When I got up t'speir aboot
His views on votes for women,
An ill-faur'd tyke, t'chuck me oot
Flew on me like a demon.*

*He tousled a' my snod back hair
'Hauns aff!', says I; 'I ware ye.'
Says he, 'I'll heave ye doon the stair
That's hoo they dae in Caurnie.*

*I've been syne t'Ru'glen toon
T'bother Mr. Haldane.
When I got up, a weel-faur'd loon
Said, 'Feth, but you're a bauld ane.'*

*He gently catched me roon the waist,
Speired if I wished a cairry;
When on the grun' my feet he placed
Says he, 'D'ye think ye'll mairry?'*

*Oh! thon's the way t'cuddly tease;
It maks ane feel sae snug. Then
When ye want a proper squeeze
Just mak' a ca' at Ru'glen.*

The first suffrage society was started in Edinburgh as early as 1867 but it was not until the beginning of the 20th century that the movement became strong in Scotland. In 1871 property owners and married women were allowed to vote in local elections. In 1881 this was extended to include all women but the right to vote in General Elections eluded

The Dundee Suffragettes on the warpath.   Dundee City Libraries.

SUFFRAGE

The right to vote became a major campaign which caught the imagination of women of all ages and backgrounds. Some men supported the cause not just vocally but by taking action. The Northern Men's Federation for Women's Suffrage was

Eunice Murray [1877-1960]:

lived all her life in the village of Cardross near Helensburgh. Third daughter of a Glasgow lawyer she was educated at St. Leonard's School, St. Andrews. In 1908, encouraged by her mother who was a keen supporter of the right to vote, she went to local meetings held by the Women's Social and Political Union in Helensburgh.

When in 1909 the breakaway Women's Freedom League was formed she began taking an active part, speaking at rallies in halls and in the open air, outside factories such as John Brown's and Singer at Clydebank and at seaside resorts on the Clyde where crowds up to 1000 would gather.

She became the secretary for all members outwith Edinburgh or Glasgow and took part in peaceful demonstrations, 'crying' meetings by ringing a bell and chalking notices on pavements.

In 1912 she took part in a march from Edinburgh to London but disliked the conditions in which she had to live and the constant noise and crowds. She also disliked the behaviour of the militant W.S.P.U..

'My type of mind could never do the things they do' she wrote in her diary.

In 1913 she was elected president of the W.F.L. in Scotland. She was vociferous in her condemnation of the Government who could provide creches during WW1 when women were needed to work to replace the men who had gone to fight, praise their efforts throughout the war yet refuse them dole money when they were dismissed in 1918. She felt that women had been shabbily treated. In 1916 she wrote

'A struggle is bound to take place between capital and labour and women's place in the labour market will suffer'.

She believed that women ought to be responsible for their own destiny and this led her to be the first woman in Scotland to stand for Parliament. This was in 1918

Bonnie Fechters ~ Women in Scotland 1900-1950

them. The Women's Social and Political Union began to be considered too militant by many women and breakaway groups were formed.

By the turn of the century the Scottish Federation of Women's Suffrage Societies included 26 organisations. In 1902 the Glasgow and West of Scotland Association for Women's Suffrage was formed, there was a Scottish Universities Women's Suffrage Union and the Scottish Women's Liberal Federation were staunch supporters. In 1905 there were branches of the National Female Franchise Association and the Catholic Women's Suffrage Society and in 1909 the largest group, the Women's Freedom League broke away from the W.S.P.U. and came into being. These were all non-violent, non party political groups. Support was also given by the Scottish Co-operative Women's Guild. A suffrage rally and pageant was held in Edinburgh in 1907 where even the bagpipes were played by women. The movement grew, drawing crowds of ordinary women at meetings in burghs and county towns as well as in cities throughout Scotland.

Women objected to the fact that they were expected to pay taxes to support a government in whose composition they had no say. The Tax Resistance League was set up with support from the Independent Labour Movement periodical, *Forward*. M.P.'s such as Keir Hardie and Tom Johnston wrote articles advocating votes for women.

There was a mix of social backgrounds within the movement: 40% of activists were from the working-class, there were many middle class supporters too and the aristocracy also lent weight to the cause. Lady Frances Balfour, sister of the Duke of Argyll and sister-in-law of the late Prime Minister was an ardent campaigner as was Ishbel, Countess of Aberdeen. Women were not all sisters under the skin however and there were fierce arguments about the differing ideas of the type of action which should be used. The Pankhursts' Women's Social and Political Union was more militant than the others and had a large following in Scotland led by the virago Flora Drummond. They were frowned upon by many women and considered to have given the movement a bad name. They were criticised for giving many M.P.'s who had pledged to support votes for women an excuse to back down and vote against the Conciliation Bill of 1912 which would have brought it about. Their actions included firing pillar boxes, stone throwing and breaking windows. Mr. Asquith, the Prime Minister on a private visit to Bannockburn found himself on the receiving end of rowdy behaviour when his car was held up and he had pepper thrown at him. He was also threatened with a dog-whip.

In 1913 another attempt was made to pass an Act of Parliament. This time although householders and wives of householders were to be enfranchised, all single women without property, who made up the bulk of the female workforce, were ignored. It also failed. On declaration of war in 1914 the movement desisted from its activities and the Pankhursts worked hard to encourage women to come forward and work in munitions and essential services to allow the men to go to fight.

In 1918 the vote was given to women over thirty who fulfilled certain property clauses. Included in

when she presented herself as an independent candidate for the Bridgeton Division of Glasgow. She failed to get elected and it was 1923 before a woman M.P. sat in the House of Commons. As a young woman Eunice was a 'bonnie fechter' and throughout her life she did her best for her community.

In 1923 she became a County Councillor in Dunbartonshire and in the same year the first president of the local Women's Rural Institute. From 1930-48 she was the president of the Dunbartonshire Federation of the W.R.I.. In 1933 she campaigned to have land for a bowling green, tennis court and sportsfield in Cardross and in 1937 when it was granted became a member of the Cardross Trust.

WW2 saw her organising amongst other things a Wings For Victory Week in Dunbartonshire at which it was hoped to raise £400,000 and which realised £964,783. She served on the executive committee of the Women's Suffrage National Aid Corps which established workrooms in Edinburgh and Glasgow for girls who lost their employment after WW1. These workshops made garments for Belgian refugees. Recognition of her good works came in 1945 with an award of M.B.E..

Not content with local affairs she was a founder member of the National Trust serving on its Council. Like her father she was interested in local history and wrote books and pamphlets. She is the author also of two of the few books written on the subject of Scottish women, which were published in the 1930's.

Those who knew her in later life might have been amazed had they known how rebellious she had been in her youth. They saw a douce, churchgoing spinster who kindly threw the first jack or served the first ball of the sports season.

She died in 1960 at Moorpark, the house she had lived in for eighty three years.

Elizabeth Dorothea Chalmers Smith [1872-1944]:

as Miss Lyness was one of the first women to graduate as a doctor from the University of Glasgow. She became involved with the Women's Social and Political Union and was not afraid of taking militant action when necessary. After an arson attempt on an empty house she and Ethel Moorhead were sent to jail in Duke Street Prison in Glasgow in 1914. They were sentenced to 8 months imprisonment. She went on hunger strike and had to be force fed. After a few days she was released on medical grounds under the Cat and Mouse Act which allowed prisoners home if they were unwell but expected them to return when better. She failed to do so voluntarily and had to be re-arrested. Her husband was minister of Calton Parish Church and could not tolerate her behaviour any longer. She left home taking her four daughters and found work at the Samaritan Hospital for Women in order to support this legislation was the right to stand as a candidate in Parliamentary elections. It was not until 1928 however that every woman gained the right to vote.

Some suffragists fought passionately for the cause, sometimes sacrificing their marriages in the process, for although many men were supportive of their ideals a few could not accept their wives', to them, outrageous behaviour.

LOCAL GOVERNMENT

In 1907 an Act was passed allowing women to be elected as town or county councillors. While some councils found that women were willing to stand for election, and were even more delighted to win, it was some time before the appearance of women in council chambers became a common feature of Scottish municipal life. In many areas as late as 1964 there were no women on the council. The fact that in Dollar, Lavinia Malcolm was quick off the mark and that decade by decade others did gain a foothold in local government was a major achievement. Some women let their own side down by not taking up their right to vote and preferring to vote for a man than a woman when the opportunity presented itself.

The National Council of Women was a broad organisation which encouraged women of all political colours to stand at local elections. The President of the International Council was the Marchioness of Aberdeen and Tenair and many of its members, particularly those who served on its committees, were titled women. Other members tried, unsuccessfully, to get women elected onto the Labour Ward Committees and to ensure their selection as candidates in local elections. At meetings of the NCW lectures were held on topics of political interest to women. In 1919 on the 11th November one lecture about Women Police and Their Work was reported in *The Glasgow Herald*.

The variety of voluntary societies and associations mentioned here shows the devotion and sense of duty which existed at this time.
Stirling Journal & Advertiser, 30/10/1919.

WHO'S WHO AMONG THE WOMEN CANDIDATES

TOWN COUNCIL

King Street Ward — Miss Grace Rosina Tasker, OBE, 22 Clarendon Place, hon. secretary and treasurer of A. and S.H. Prisoners of War Fund and of Stirlingshire Work Depot; member of Education Authority; member of Committee of Child Welfare; staff-captain of Girl Guides.

Port Street Ward — Miss Catherine Turnbull, 3 Port Street, vice-president of Stirling Girls' Club, and one of the chief workers among the girls; member of the Juvenile Tribunal for out-of-work Donations.

Cowane Street Ward — Mrs Mary Caroline Macnab, 24 Park Terrace, president of the Railway Mission; managed the Communal Kitchen at the Corn Exchange.

St. Ninians Ward — Mrs Mary Fraser Smith, 20 Clarendon Place, secretary of the National Council of Women; Member of the Stirling Burgh national Health Insurance Committee.

PARISH COUNCIL

King Street Ward — Miss Louisa Caw, 1 Royal Gardens, acting sister for five years at the Stirling Military Hospital.

Port Street Ward — Miss Marion Mitchell, 10 Pitt Terrace, daughter of the late Sheriff Mitchell; superintendent of the Stirlingshire Work Depot; member of the Committee of the Girls' Industrial School, The Girls' Club, and the Girl Guides.

Cowane Street Ward — Miss Maragaret D. McJannet, Woodlands, worked under the RedCross at Southwood V.A.D. Hospital, and at the Stirlingshire Work Depot.

---

them. In 1930 she set up a private practice in Dennistoun and eventually was divorced from her husband. Her daughters became doctors but she was never allowed to see her two sons again. She died in 1944.

Mrs Lavinia Laing Malcolm:

In November 1907 she became the first woman town councillor in Scotland. She was elected in Dollar having already served as a member of the School Board and the Parish Council. She supported the non-violence campaign of the suffragists and was Vice President of Clackmannan and Kinross Women's Liberal Association. In 1913 she was elected the first woman provost in Scotland.

Grace Mary Tasker:

In 1919 when Miss Grace Tasker became the first lady member of Stirlingshire Education Authority, *The Stirling Journal and Advertiser* wrote

'After she loses her sense of awe for the brilliant men around her in the meeting room Miss Tasker should prove a useful member for she demonstrated her administrative ability during the war as honorary secretary of the Stirlingshire Work Depot [She was War Work Parties Coordinator for Stirlingshire] and worked for the Argyll and Sutherland Highlanders Prisoner of War Fund.'

She gained a seat on Stirling Town Council in 1919 and on the same day Miss Catherine Turnbull, a manageress of a local boot and shoe shop, was also elected. *The Stirling Journal and Advertiser* once again excelled itself. They reported that

'The work of the Council should not suffer in any way by this departure from the norm.'; and about her award of M.B.E. it states: *' in her case [it was] thoroughly well deserved whatever may be said of some of its other recipients.'*

She became a bailie and the Council's first lady magistrate in 1924. She was also active on the National Council of Women.

Unionist Burns Supper, 1926. Mrs L. A. Luke, chairman, standing at the front.
Strathkelvin District LIbraries.

Janet Luke [1882-1975]:

was born in Thurso but came to Chryston, North Lanarkshire in 1910 on marriage. She served on Cadder Parish Council for many years before becoming Chairman of the 9th District of Lanarkshire Cadder Area Subcommittee where she was

Bonnie Fechters ~ Women in Scotland 1900-1950

NATIONAL GOVERNMENT

Service in national government was denied to women until the Representation of the People Act 1918 which extended the franchise to some but still not all women and allowed those who qualified to stand for Parliament. The first woman Member of Parliament from Scotland belonged to the aristocracy. Women found it difficult to gain selection as candidates and rarely could rely on a safe seat. Often other women on local branch committees were as vociferous in their rejection as any man. Over the years because of the historic workings of the House of Commons women have continued to find it difficult to even consider putting themselves forward. This, rather than lack of talent or capability, is the reason so few women become M.P.'s.

Mary Ewart's attitude is typical; talent, enthusiasm, even a strong political belief are not enough for women to sacrifice their families to satisfy their own ambitions. The Parliamentary system of unsocial hours, being in London through the week, travelling hundreds of miles each week then arriving home to attend to surgeries and meetings in the constituency can only be carried on by those either privileged enough to have professional help or who are unshackled by family ties. Occasionally women were offered the seat on the death of their husband who was the sitting M.P.. This was however to ensure loyalty to his memory from the voters rather than deliberate selection of women for their own sake. In the House of Lords progress was even slower and it was not until 1958 that women were admitted to the upper chamber.

---

an active and vociferous member on behalf of women. This brought her into conflict with a Mr. Auld who clearly resented her position and he took every opportunity to make digs at her expense. When she suggested that a woman might stand for a vacancy in the Baillieston Ward of Lanark County Council he said that the people of Baillieston had more sense and after similar comments when she complained he said, *'If you can't take it, resign.'* which made her even more determined to become a county councillor.

In 1930 she stood unsuccessfully as a candidate for Chryston and later that year was asked to stand for co-option the choice being between herself and a gentleman. She was turned down. Eventually she was elected for the Garrowhill Ward and served for a number of years. She also became a J.P. She was active in voluntary work, being President of the Women's Voluntary Service in Lanarkshire, President of the local Red Cross Society and a tireless worker for the Earl Haig Fund. She was chairman of the West of Scotland Unionist Association and she also served on its Scottish Executive Council. With her husband she was active in the Chryston Young Unionist Association for which they organised and produced musical operettas. In 1926 the Women's Unionist Association held a Burns Supper in Chryston and decided to form a Women's Burns Club. This was sacrilege to many men who considered anything to do with the bard a male preserve. Her public service covered many years and she was awarded the O.B.E.

W.V.S. Senior Ladies Christmas party with Provost Mary Ewart.
Hamilton District Libraries

Mary Ewart [1911-]:

took an early interest in politics having read her father's trade union material as a child in Coatbridge. She married David Ewart and moved to Hamilton. The Labour Party, Ladies Section held meetings in the Miners Hall in Cadzow Street and she joined up. During WW2 she worked at the Ministry of War Transport. She was persuaded to stand for election to Hamilton Town Council and her success brought her the honour of being its first woman councillor. In 1953 she was appointed Provost, the youngest and the first woman.

Well thought of and respected by all parties it was suggested that she stand against Winifred Ewing, S.N.P., at the 1966 General Election. She declined.

'I had a husband and two children at home and did not want to leave them to the wolves. I wanted to see that the children got a chance in life. All children are entitled to that.'

She remained at home but served the public well by being chairman of Hamilton and Motherwell Hospital Board and deputy chairman of the Scottish Special Housing Association.

In an article in the Hamilton Advertiser, to mark her 80th birthday she is quoted as saying

'I was just an ordinary housewife who was trying to do her best to help ordinary men and women.'

Mary lives in Hamilton where she still enjoys a good discussion with young people about politics.

Katherine Marjory, Duchess of Atholl [1874-1960]:

was Scotland's first woman M.P. At 49 years of age she took her seat for Kinross and West Perth in the 1923 General Election along with another seven women from other parts of the U.K. [3 Conservative, 3 Labour and 2 Liberal]. In a 73% poll she gained the seat for the Conservatives and Unionists from the Liberals with a majority of 150.

She remained in the House until 1938 being the first woman to hold a ministerial post. She was Parliamentary Secretary to the Board of Education from 1924-1929. She resigned from

Bonnie Fechters ~ Women in Scotland 1900-1950

Parliamentary office because she opposed Chamberlain believing that a stand should have been made against Hitler. She was defeated when she stood as an independent in the by-election.

As Marchioness of Tullibardine she was a supporter of the Scottish Women's National Anti-suffrage League which was founded by the Duchess of Montrose and in 1913 was vice-president of the Dundee branch.. She believed in the feminist movement and claimed for women most of the freedoms which were the goals of the suffragists but she felt that women should use their influence to force their husbands to act on their behalf. She also believed that it was the duty of married women and those who had led sheltered lives to learn about the social evils, especially poverty and do what they could to relieve them. She had been President of Perthshire Women's Unionist Association from 1908-1919 but was known as the 'Red Duchess' for her support of the Spanish Government during the Spanish Civil War in 1936. She was Honorary Colonel of the Duke's regiment, the Scottish Horse.

During WW1 she was commandant of the Voluntary Aid Detachment Hospital which was set up in her home, Blair Castle, Blair Atholl. She was involved in the District Nursing Association and was president of the county Red Cross Society. She held honorary degrees from universities, wrote books and always took a lively interest in topics of the day. She died in 1960, eighteen years after her husband.

Jennie Lee [1904 - 1988]:

was the daughter of a Fife miner. She was Labour M.P. for North Lanark from 1929 - 1931. She married Aneurin Bevan but in true Scottish tradition kept her own name. In 1930 she wanted to introduce Family Allowances ,an idea which had previously been mooted by the Scottish Women's Conference of the Scottish Trades Union Congress, and asked Philip Snowden, the Chancellor, how much it would cost the State to give 5/- per week to all children under 15 years of age. His reply was £140,000,000 which killed the idea stone dead. Again in 1930 she challenged the fact that women were being denied welfare benefit if they refused domestic work.

'The Labour Exchange is perhaps unwittingly being made an instrument in reducing the status and very often the wages of women once they become unemployed. Domestic service would not be so unpopular if it paid a decent wage and was an insured occupation.'

She was a Minister in the Labour Government from 1964 - 1970 and was made a life peeress in 1970.

Margaret Herbison (above) [1907 -]:

affectionately known as Peggy has lived in Shotts all her life. She became a teacher after taking her Highers at Bellshill Academy. She taught for 15 years before being elected in 1945 as the second woman Labour M.P. for North Lanarkshire. Thereafter her service in the House of Commons covered 25 years. She rose quickly to become a member of the Cabinet and held a number of important posts. She was joint Under Secretary of State in the Scottish Office 1950-1951,

'one of the highlights of my career. I was in charge of the Home Office brief, police, prisons and health and education.'

In 1949 she attended the first European Parliament, as the only female delegate. In 1956/57 she was chairman of the Labour Party. In Government from 1964 - 67, as Minister of Pensions and National Insurance, she was responsible in 1966 for setting up the Ministry of Social Security under Harold Wilson. In 1970 she became the first woman to represent the Queen as Lord High Commissioner to the General Assembly of the Church of Scotland. That same year she was elected Scotswoman of the Year.

Katherine, Baroness Elliot of Harwood (right) [1903-]:

In 1958 four peeresses were allowed to take up their seats in the House of Lords for the first time. Amongst them Katherine, the daughter of Charles Tennant, the chemical entrepreneur. Her sympathies were with the Liberal Party but as no Liberal candidate was standing she agreed to help in her brother-in-law's campaign to win a Conservative seat in Leicester in 1924. She came into contact with the Conservative M.P. for Lanark, Walter Elliot, whose first wife had died tragically on honeymoon in 1919.

As a Liberal, Katherine spoke at meetings and on such an occasion in Edinburgh in 1934, Walter proposed to her before she took the platform. The National Farmers Union took up a subscription for a wedding present at 1/- per head from 40,000 members. A porter in the New Club, the shrine of conservatism in Edinburgh, quipped to Walter

'Weel, Mr. Elliot, you'll be leading her from darkness to light.'

During WW2 she ran the recruiting office in London for the Women's Land Army and she and her husband turned Harwood House in Hawick into a safe haven for Edinburgh schoolchildren. From 1954-57 she acted as a delegate to the United Nations Organisation and was given an O.B.E. in 1958. In 1956 her husband was Lord High Commissioner for that year's General Assembly of the Church of Scotland and she enjoyed entertaining the great and mighty and their wives, as hostess of Holyrood Palace.

Bonnie Fechters ~ Women in Scotland 1900-1950

INDUSTRIAL ACTION

Scottish women were not always the docile workforce of the stereotype. They might have wanted to be respectable, temperate and well thought of but they were equally capable of speaking out and fighting against injustice. Women were not just the teamakers but often the instigators of industrial action.

Strike Song: Mary Brooksbank: Dundee. [Tune: Vote, vote vote.]

*We are out for higher wages
As we have the right to do.
And we'll never be content
Till we get oor ten per cent
For we have a right to live
As well as you.*

Singer Sewing Machine Company:

In 1911 a strike initiated by women workers in the polishing department against an increased workload without increased pay saw 380 out of 400 women walk out. 2000 women in other departments came out in sympathy and the strike gained the support also of male workers and spread throughout the works. The women were not organised but acted independently although the strike gained the backing of the Industrial Workers of Great Britain, a union whose members encouraged women to take an active part and did not treat them as inferior, unlike the S.T.U.C. and the Glasgow Trades Council neither of which lent support

Many women took part in the three week dispute, picketing, demonstrating and attending meetings. Two were on the strike committee and one sat at the negotiating table. The American owners of the famous sewing machine works were fiercely anti-trade union and victimisation and sackings took place including that of the two women who stood up for their beliefs. It was 1963 before the first forewoman was appointed.

An advertisement for Singer sewing machines. c1913 Katy Gardiner.

Mary MacArthur & Kate McLean, (3rd & 2nd right), STUC 1911, Dundee. NLS

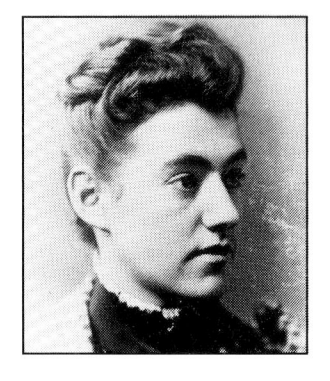

Jane Rae (above) [1872-1959]:

was 39 when she became politically active. She was a ringleader in the Singer strike of 1911 and was sacked afterwards. A suffragist as well as a member of the Temperance Movement, the Anti-war Movement and the Co-operative Movement, her involvement with politics began as a Liberal, then she joined the I.L.P. and became secretary of the local Clydebank branch in 1913.

She loved getting up on a soap box and preaching to anyone who would listen. Later she stood as a Labour candidate for the Town Council and served from 1922-1928 becoming a Bailie. Not afraid to be seen, her campaigns were colourful with bell ringing and painted slogans, a trick learned during her days as a suffragist.

She married at 56 and went to live in Australia where she gave up politics. During WW2 she was in the Channel Islands and was harassed by the Germans because of her past reputation. She returned to Clydebank and died there aged 87 in 1959.

Mary MacArthur [1880-1921]:

was a well educated journalist who worked for a Conservative newspaper. In 1895 she was assigned to cover a meeting of women trade unionists.

'I went to a meeting at Ayr to write a skit on the proceedings. Going to scoff, I remained to pray. I became impressed with the truth and meaning of the Labour Movement.'

Her father was a draper and she became interested in the Shop Assistant's Union.. From 1903- 1921 she was secretary of the Women's Trade Union League and a founder member and secretary from 1906 -1921 of the National Federation of Women Workers. In 1906 she also worked for the Anti-Sweating League which established wages boards and set minimum wage rates. In 1919 they demanded equal pay for equal work.

She was a delegate for the National Federation of Women Workers to the Scottish Trades Union Conference in 1909 and spoke out against the Truck System

Bonnie Fechters ~ Women in Scotland 1900-1950

Fishing Net Workers; Kilbirnie:

In 1913 women workers in several netmaking works in Kilbirnie went on strike for 21 weeks. They were members of the National Federation of Women Workers and the organiser was Miss Kate McLean, who was the NFWW delegate to the Scottish Trades Union Conference where she served on its Parliamentary Committee from 1911-1913.

The fishing net workers wanted an increase in their payment per net and trade union recognition. Not everyone went on strike and in protest against the despised blacklegs an effigy was burnt at a rally in Beith attended by over 8000 men and women. Police protection was needed at the gates of the works both morning and night.

Six networkers were charged with disorderly conduct in Kilmarnock Sheriff Court under the Conspiracy and Protection of Property Act 1875, sect 7, on 19th May 1913. Four were found guilty and ordered to pay a fine of 30/- or 5 days imprisonment.

The strikers were supported by the M.P. George Barnes. James Maxton and Patrick Dolan also spoke at meetings. George Barnes supported equal pay for equal work. The women are reported as singing a 'war' song '*We're all going the same way home*' before each meeting. From collections taken at meetings, concerts and dances a strike pay of 7/6 was given to the women who had been out for 12 weeks and 5/- to those who had recently joined in.

The women were supported by a wide range of men's unions and in August there was a partial settlement by the firm of John Watt & Sons offering 4d per net and this was accepted. Some workers returned and this led to violence, including stone throwing. There was fighting between strike sympathisers and returning workers and men were mobbed for letting their daughters return to work.

Bailie McKerrel of Kilmarnock, acting as negotiator with the employers, brought about a general settlement in September which resulted in a rise of 1/6 per week for most women. At a public meeting he said

'That in future members of the Union should not interfere with non-members either at their work or outside, but if they wanted to persuade non-members to join...they should do so in their homes or in private.'

Kate McLean of the National Federation of Women Workers spoke of her intention to recruit more net workers into the Union. Her targets were Beith and those on the east coast.

Other strikes took place: fisherwomen at Grimsby in 1910 over excessive hours of work, thread mill workers in East Renfrewshire in 1911. Dundee mill girls struck in 1912/1913 and when Forfarshire textile workers were offered increases of 5% for men, 2% for women the latter stayed out and won their case. Dressmakers and milliners came out in 1917 and the waitresses in dispute in Glasgow in 1920 took advertising space in the press. The nurses threatened to strike in 1939 over pay and conditions and women were again involved in the Singer strike of 1957.

The Singer Strike of 1957.
Clydebank District Libraries.

---

which allowed employers to give tokens in lieu of money. These tokens had to be spent in shops owned by the employers. She wanted to make all fines and direct deductions from workers' wages illegal. She remained a delegate until her marriage to a Dunfermline miner.

She was a member of the War Emergency Workers National Committee and was defeated as a Labour candidate in 1918 becoming a member of the National Executive Council of the Labour Party in 1919/20.

She became Honorary Secretary for the Central Committee on Women's Employment of the National Federation of Women Workers. Given £500,000 by the Government she set up schemes in 'domestic subjects' and 'women's trades'. This perpetuated the stereotype rather than opening up opportunities in a wider field. In 1920 she argued that a baby was more wonderful than a machine gun and that women would eventually gain political power but opposed the French idea that women should be allowed to take their babies to work with them. She believed in equal pay for equal work.

Margaret Irwin (above) [1857-1940]:

was born in Broughty Ferry the daughter of a ship's captain. She became influential in the trade union movement and believed in the benefits of federation. She emphasised that Scotland needed its own unions not merely branches of a national body because conditions and types of work in Scotland were different. She was a suffragist and was secretary of the Glasgow and West of Scotland Association for Women's Suffrage serving on the executive committee until 1907.

Originally secretary to the Glasgow Council for Women's Trades, she became secretary to the Scottish Council for Women's Trades and of the Women's Protective and Provident League the first trade union for women formed originally in England in 1874. When a Royal

Bonnie Fechters ~ Women in Scotland 1900-1950

Carrying out ideals such as equal pay was not always feasible as this excerpt from the *Kirkintilloch Herald* of 9/1/1918 shows.

> **Stepps Women's Equal Rights Society met on Monday evening to consider Miss C's complaint that the Society had failed to support her in her endeavour to introduce its principles into her business.**
>
> **Miss C. reminded them that they had given their tacit promise to support her. In spite of the fact that her goods were of the best quality and a price consistent of fair business they had persistently passed the door and patronised the most notorious sweating firms in Glasgow.**
>
> **She had just learned that several warehouses in Glasgow conducted on the same lines [i.e. paying equal wages] were insolvent, and if certain of them closed their doors she would have to do the same.**
>
> **Mrs. D.**
>
> **May I be permitted to explain why I have been compelled to deal in Glasgow. We require even the few shillings saved. When we married my husband had £2 per week. His firm joined the new movement and so far equalised their salaries by giving the girl clerks £1 per week and reducing my husband's wage to 30/-.**
>
> **Mrs. E.**
>
> **We seem to be involved in the very old process of increasing the blanket at the top by sewing on a piece cut from the bottom. My two sons are working for 75% of their previous wage while my daughter earns 25% more.**

RENT STRIKES

This was a non-industrial based struggle which took place in Glasgow in 1915 and in Clydebank from 1920 -1928.

Women initiated the action and resisted eviction like animals protecting their young. Not all the women were politically active but they saw the raising of rents without improvements as an injustice. Tactics were discussed in houses and not necessarily in meeting rooms.

Factors took tenants to court only to be confounded by the discovery of a legal loophole. Factors were supposed to give a notice of removal before a notice of increase could be valid and as they had failed to do this the Sheriff upheld the tenants' claim. Nevertheless eviction remained a real threat. Janet Hyslop, one of the leaders of the housewives remembers

'I had a big bell. And I just ran out and rang it and everything was dropped. We met the Sheriff Officers. Sometimes we discussed the matter with them through the letterbox. We didnae let them in the hoose.'
From: Rent Strike, Sean Damer, 1982.

The women exchanged houses screwing another nameplate to the door to confuse the Sheriff Officers. They spoke at street corners, attended meetings, ran socials to

Rent Strike, 1912. Householders evicted at Dalmuir.
Clydebank Distric Libraries.

Commission on Labour was conducting an enquiry into working conditions of women in Scotland she was invited to be a member of the sub-commission.

In 1897 she is credited as being a founder member of the Scottish Trades Union Congress. The first meeting was at Falkirk in 1896 when she was elected secretary of the Provisional Committee. Its aims were to prevent strikes and lockouts, to promote harmony and to avoid needless friction. She tried to get male trade unionists to support women's suffrage and also equal pay for women but they felt that there were other matters which were more pressing. At the 1st Congress which was held in Glasgow she topped the poll for membership of the Parliamentary Committee. Considering that she was the only woman delegate standing this was a magnificent achievement for a middle-class girl and recognised her wide experience of working conditions. She was offered the post of permanent secretary but declined because she feared that at this early stage there would be prejudice against the Congress if the post was filled by a woman and also turned down the invitation to become chairman for the same reason. Her organisational skills were excellent and her energy amazing.

She was a regular member of deputations to Whitehall and Westminster and encouraged other women to become involved.

She was awarded the CBE in 1927

Marion Henery [1910 -]:

was born in Cambuslang. Her father was a stonemason and her mother came from Skye. They lived in a red sandstone tenement in a two room and kitchen flat in a very respectable area.

Bonnie Fechters ~ Women in Scotland 1900-1950

raise funds. The butchers in Dalmuir gave stock and the women made soup which was taken to those who were evicted. The Council housed the homeless, first in tents then in converted railway carriages. Support came from the Scottish Co-operative Women's Guild, I.L.P., the Women's Labour League and the Women's Section of the British Legion. The memory which remains is of the unity of women fighting a basic prolonged injustice rather than a political struggle.

The Scottish Co-operative Women's Guild gave many women the confidence to speak in public and to learn and discuss.

In Lanarkshire there were 51 branches with over 3000 members mainly in the mining and industrial districts. In Glasgow the Kinning Park branch was the oldest and took part, with its banners, in marches against the Means Test and other political rallies.

'I found the Guild and found something fresh to listen to while there and something to think about all the week. I was not used to working women managing their meetings. I had attended mothers' meetings, where ladies came and lectured on the domestic affairs in the workers' homes that it was impossible for them to understand.'
Stirling Women's Oral History Project 1988.

The Women's Labour League was founded in 1908 by Margaret Ethel Macdonald, wife of the Prime Minister. Miss Taylor, herself a suffragist, was organising secretary and was also a member of the Independent Labour party. The League helped out at elections, provided speakers for the Right To Work Bill, fought destitution by providing shelters and was complementary to the I.L.P..

In the recession of the 1930's hundreds of men and women were unable to find work and had to rely on the dole. Even those in employment suffered as wages and hours were being cut. Hunger Marches were a protest against the Means Test which was seen as a ploy to remove people from the Register of Unemployment. Many marches took place during the period 1922 - 1936, both within Scotland and across the border to London. In 1928 100 women and children walked from Broxburn to Edinburgh.

Oh why are we marching?
Oh why are we marching?
Oh why are we marching?
Oh why?, why? why?
The reason is the Means Test.
The reason is the Means Test.
The reason is the Means Test.
That's why! why! why!.
[tune; Come all ye faithful]

In 1943 Women For Westminster was set up. This was a cross party group, many members of which had campaigned for the vote for women. Its aim was to encourage women to put themselves forward for selection as candidates at the General Election and to try to obtain a 50% representation for women. The organisation collapsed in 1945.

In 1947 the Scottish Housewives Association was established, its symbol being scissors cutting red tape. It was against the slowness of the Government in making necessities available after wartime rationing which for many items continued until 1951. In the 1950's it opposed the fluoridation scheme for tap water.

The Peace Movement had existed since WW1 when women like Marjorie Newbold, a progressive schoolteacher from Ayrshire worked actively to promote the Anti-War Movement, as did Jane Rae of Clydebank. Others were members of the Anti-Conscription League or the No-Conscription Fellowship. These were mixed groups. In the 1930s the Scottish Trades Union Congress held a Scottish Peace Conference which was well attended by women and in the 1950's many women took part in demonstrations against the siting of nuclear armaments and became members of the Scottish Council for Nuclear Disarmament. Another group known as the Moral Rearmament Society Players toured Scotland acting out dramas which supported their cause.

The names of the majority of women and women's groups mentioned in this chapter may not be recorded in the major biographies, not even in the history books. That is not their fault and they cannot be accused of inactivity in political matters in their widest sense.

'My sister Mary was the oldest of the family. The headmaster sent for my father to ask him to allow her to stay on at school. She was so bright but she had to take days off to look after the weans on washing day because mother went to the washhouse.'
Marion went to Skerry's College in Glasgow when she left school to take shorthand, typing and commercial bookkeeping.
'I wasn't keen to become an office worker. It was just one of the things that you did from a working-class home. It never occurred to me that I should maybe think about university. It just didn't come into the scheme of things with working-class people at that time.'
Once qualified she became personal assistant to Willie Allan of the United Mineworkers of Scotland. In 1931 she attended meetings of the Young Communist League and although not at first politically involved she started speaking at branches. In 1932 she was a member of the Women's Contingent in the Hunger March, a separate demonstration from the men's. Many of the women had no political affiliation. Marion was not herself unemployed but she wanted to march in sympathy. She wore a navy blue skirt and blazer, lisle stockings, a woolly jumper, the cobbler added thick soles to her shoes, a haversack and off she went. She remembers that she had no nightdress and that the reception was better in some places than others. Often they were put up in the Poorhouse. They marched 16 - 20 miles per day for 10 days. The Liberals offered support and food en route. She came home by train which was paid for by the National Union of Mine Workers.

In 1933 she gave up her job and went to the Soviet Union. Returning to Scotland in 1935 she married a miner from Blantyre who went to work at the West Lothian 'Dardanelles' pit which was notorious for accidents.

Bonnie Fechters ~ Women in Scotland 1900-1950

Women ~ *the new discovery*

War brought women into their own. As men headed off to join up in 1914 women were called upon to take their place. Necessity made them a valuable commodity or as Eunice Murray, the suffragist called them - in a pamphlet which she wrote haranguing the Government - the New Discovery.

WW1 brought fears that if women made a success of work previously reserved for men then after the war men would not only have to compete for jobs but would be offered the lower rates now paid to women. Women could not win. If they agreed to accept lower rates they were threatening male wages and at the same time equal pay or wages which gave them independence challenged men. Traditional attitudes that women were inferior, delicate, not mechanically minded and that their place was in the home were under attack. In this respect women faced the opposition of the male dominated ranks of both the employers and trade unions.

Dilution of labour was the description given to the employment of women in munitions, railways and shipyards during 1914-1918. Life for women in Scotland was changed for ever by this experience. Coping without the support of men gave them a new confidence in their own abilities. Suddenly it was acceptable for married women to work. Some enlightened firms set up creches and nurseries. Many servicemen's wives welcomed these and took the opportunity to supplement the weekly Government allowance of 13/- plus 2/- for each child. Women flocked from domestic service delighted to escape the drudgery and discipline and to earn regular money.

Women stokers, Singer Manufacturing Co. WW1
Clydebank District Libraries

They discovered a new world where they could go about unchaperoned. Some were daring enough to smoke and drink although many public houses refused entry to unaccompanied women and as late as the 1950's some did not permit them to sit or stand at the bar. Alcohol was frowned on by many women and the behaviour of these younger women with money to burn was looked down on by the majority. While goods were still available fashionable clothes were snapped up, even fox furs and other luxury items according to one report. Other women became very patriotic donating as much as they could towards medical equipment. Knitting and sewing needles were kept busy and Red Cross parcels for the troops were made up containing books, sweets and tobacco. As war dragged on shortages became severe and food was rationed as it also was in World War Two.

Textile mills were amongst the first firms to convert to war work. Many women were already employed there and they changed over to the weaving of khaki cloth to be made into uniforms. Women in shoe factories had also to work flat out to produce army boots.

CONSCRIPTION

Conscription of unmarried women aged 16-30 was introduced in 1916. Many middle-class women went into shops, offices, factories or the various services, nurses and doctors volunteered to go abroad and working-class women chose munitions and factories but there was no hard and fast division by social class. During WW2 from 1940 married women were conscripted if they did not have young children while women in civvy street again played a major part in 'manning' industry, working in factories, working on the land and running businesses to help the war effort.

Many joined up becoming plotters of aeroplanes, office workers, drivers or mechanics. Some even had dangerous jobs working on secret missions or flew aeroplanes but not fighters or bombers.

Voluntary work was carried out in both wars by women from all levels of society. War helped to even out the old social divisions. Many well-off people or owners of mansions offered their properties for the duration of the war as hospitals or to house evacuated schools. Some houses were requisitioned for these purposes as were hotels.

MUNITIONS

David Lloyd George became Minister for Munitions in 1915 on the passing of the Munitions Act which encouraged firms to convert to war production. Shipyards, railway work-shops, engineering works turned part of their premises over to the national effort. By 1918 50% of munition workers were women earning good money.

In Inverness, A.I. Welders employed women and had to instal

special facilities for them. In Springburn the North British Locomotive Company dedicated two new buildings to the output of shells. One was called 'Mons' the other 'Marne' after these battles. In 1916, 683 women and 313 men were employed at N.B. Locomotives and by 1918 there were 1136 women and 405 men. Foremen and toolsetters were all men. There were no industrial disputes and accidents were rare. Nevertheless the firm employed two industrial nurses, one on dayshift the other on nightshift.

At these same works sea mines with electrically welded seams were manufactured entirely by women. Pill boxes [cages to hold two men] which were intended to be dug into the ground, military bridges, machine tools and artificial limbs were also made there; and the last were in great demand as the casualties grew.

The Dilution of Labour Act 1916 allowed women to work on building locomotives. This had always been regarded as men's work. The Act was bitterly opposed by time-served men. The Clyde Commission for the Dilution of Labour was set up and controlled the 14,000 women workers in 150 of the 300 controlled works in the Clyde area, 'all with satisfactory results'. Some employers were unhappy at having to employ women and trade unions were afraid that women would prove too successful and steal the jobs from the men.

They were also opposed to women receiving training as this would encourage them to continue working after the war. The Clyde Workers Committee was fanatically anti-women and was eventually suppressed by the Government with 10 of the leaders deported.

The terms substitution and dilution were derogatory and implied inferiority. As we have already seen this was typical of the attitude of male employers and trade unionists alike. Not all employers were as considerate as N.B. Loco. Many seemed unaware of the dangerous material which their workforce was handling. Some women munitions workers were exposed to chemicals which earned them the nickname of canaries.

A Stirling woman remembers.

'I was called up to a factory, a filling station in Stoke in 1916. I was travelling in the train with two girls from Buckie who worked at Radway Green. I heard hair raising stories about filling stations, about T.N.T. turning your skin yellow. So I went to the Labour Exchange in Stoke and said to the manageress "I'm not joining that lot".'
Stirling Women's Oral History Project, 1988

She got a job putting shells down a chute and later was transferred to an office job.

WW2

Again in 1942 women were conscripted into munitions. At the Admiralty Torpedo Factory in Alexandria, Dunbartonshire, women from various backgrounds found themselves having to adapt to factory life. They worked 12 hour shifts: 8am - 8pm and 8pm - 8am with an hour for lunch and half an hour for tea. They stood all day in a confined space. It was noisy and airless. They wore turbans and long brown dresses.

One driller recalls, *'I didn't know what the parts were for. We never saw the whole thing.'* Another filed washers all day and found the work boring. They earned 45/- for a 5 day week less National Insurance and had to take their turn of firewatching.

SHIPYARDS

Marion MacLean [1898-] still lives in Greenock. She is now 95 but remembers how as a young girl of sixteen she entered the shipyard for the first time.

'We walked up several stairs into this great big place, three of us were put to a bench and we made portable lamps. We put in the flex and made them up for the men working in the bowels of the ships which were out in the water. We were taught what to do and felt very important. We started at 6a.m. then later at 8a.m. towards the end of the war. We were put off when the men came back although we were good workers. They gave us a lamp with our name on it as a souvenir.'
Personal interview. Greenock 1994.

RAILWAYS

by tradition had always employed men and boys. When in 1915 they wanted to release more men for the fighting, women were recruited as 'substitutes'. It was considered impracticable to use them as engine

1, 2 and 3 Women munition workers at the North British Locomotive Co. Ltd., Glasgow. 1914-18.
4. Women workers at the Naval Construction Works, Dalmuir. 1918

Bonnie Fechters ~ Women in Scotland 1900-1950

drivers, firemen or shunters. The Glasgow and South Western Railway Company in 1916 increased its women workers from 442 to 1095, women clerks making up a large percentage of this number.

A weight allowance on luggage was introduced as women porters could not cope with extra heavy weights but it was not the women's lack of strength alone that aroused criticism nor their initial inefficiency at their job.

> 'At smaller stations where the male porter had not only looked after the passengers and dealt with luggage of whatever bulk but could fill up his time with shunting, lighting signal-lamps etc. a woman is clearly not an adequate substitute.' Another comment was 'The average girl or woman is generally more ready to settle down to routine work to which she may find herself allocated and not only does not seek for the opportunities to fill temporarily the more important posts which are so welcome to an aspiring youth but rather shrinks from assuming responsibilities she may regard as beyond her powers. For these reasons....she is of less value to a company.'

British Railways and the Great War. E.A. Pratt, 1921.

It may also have been the fact that at the outset of war the National Union of Railwaymen demanded assurances that these jobs should be returned to men after the war and the women dismissed as 'their value is not equal to that of men in corresponding grades and positions.'

Women worked as ticket clerks, collectors, porters, inspectors, cleaners and telegraphists. They adopted dungarees for the more arduous work of van washing, crane driving, loading and checking and work in the engine sheds. Some women had more unusual jobs as horse handlers, billiard markers, lamplighters, letter sorters, canal bridge and lock keepers.

During WW2 in Scotland the London, Midland and Scottish Railway Company had 50% of women employees acting as porters while others were on parcel vans, labouring, cleaning engines or working as stable hands and dining car attendants and clerks.

Women sorting waste paper.
British Railways and the Great War. E.A. Pratt 1921.

Women did every job under the sun. They were posties, delivered milk, cleaned chimneys and windows, became lift attendants, shopwalkers and barmaids.

One of the tragedies of war is that many women are widowed very young and others will never have the chance to marry. Married women whose husbands did survive were encouraged to replenish the population by having more children. Because women served throughout the U.K. many met and married men from a wider area and often left Scotland to set up home elsewhere. The most frustrating thing for women was that as soon as the war was over they were expected to creep back into their houses and stay there.

In her pamphlet '*Women - The New Discovery*' Eunice Murray lambasts this attitude.

> 'Men will speedily forget the fine work done by women and will think not upon what she has done but that there she is employed at his job, a competitor with him. His natural instinct will be to reject her.'

Women had to fight to be allowed to train; apprenticeship was closed to them by the protectionist attitude of the craft unions. After WW1 in the slump of the 1920's women were again dismissed on marriage. Women were driven into domestic service. If they refused such work they lost their entitlement to unemployment benefit. As a result there were more servants in 1930 than in 1921. The Sex Disqualification [Removal] Act 1919 forbade women with the exception of nurses to work nightshifts At the same time however there was a baby boom and

What did you do in the war granny?

Ysabel Alexander (Left):

*I arrived at Greenwich Naval College nervous but excited. I was on my own, my life lay ahead, I was fit, fancy free and ready for anything. After passing stringent physical and mental tests I now had my uniform. I was a Wren.
I got used to the various noises made by fellow Wrens in their bunk beds, many of them wearing steel jaws in their hair which produced tight waves by morning. After training I was posted to Campbeltown to a submarine base as Mess Caterer for the Officers' Mess in The Argyll Arms.
I served in Lancashire, Acharacle, Felixstow and Inveraray where the camp was in Nissen Huts. The washing and toilet facilities were primitive. Access was along an unlit, muddy path and even torches were not allowed.
Entertainment National Service Association stars came to entertain us and we catered for greats such as Sir Harry Lauder and Evelyn Laye. I was commissioned and posted to Ronaldsay Naval Air Station, Orkney where I met King George VI and Queen Elizabeth. One lift I got from there was terrifying. I had to crouch in the bomb rack gazing hypnotised at the panel of nobs in front of me. One touch would have opened the glass doors releasing me instead of a bomb.
Recently one of my grand-children asked what I did in the war and the eldest replied.
'Walked about in uniform looking glamorous and entertained the officers. Nothing could be further from the truth. Although on the day war ended I married one.'*

Now Mrs Sandie Shaw living in Barrassie. Personal interview, 1993.

Bonnie Fechters ~ Women in Scotland 1900-1950

more teachers, health visitors and social workers were appointed. The majority of such jobs went to qualified women who earned 75% of the wage paid to a man. In 1944 teachers were allowed to marry and keep on teaching because there was a national shortage.

We wore what we'd got

MILITARY SERVICE:

Women volunteered for military service in 1914 at the outbreak of WW1. They were needed to keep the administration, maintenance and support services going when men were sent to the Front. This was a major social upheaval as most women had never had so much freedom before.

Early in the war The Women's Legion had a Military Cooking Section and a Military Driving Section in which women could volunteer to serve. In 1917 the WAAC [Women's Army Auxiliary Corps] came into being. Members wore a khaki uniform. Some served in France as cooks and waitresses. In that year a doctor in the WAAC earned less than she would have in civvy street and less than male army doctors. In 1918 the name was changed to QMAAC [Queen Mary's Army Auxiliary Corps].

In November 1917 the WRNS [Women's Royal Naval Service] was formed but was disbanded in 1919 after the Armistice. In 1918 both the Royal Air Force and the Women's Royal Air Force were created from an amalgamation of several units concerned with flying. The WRAF was also disbanded in 1919 but its nursing service continued and in 1923 became Princess Mary's RAF Nursing Service.

In 1938 in anticipation of WW2 the ATS [Auxiliary Territorial Service] and the RAF/ATS reformed becoming in 1939 the WAAF [Women's Auxiliary Air Force]. In 1941 single women aged 19-30 were conscripted unless working in factories. Many opted to serve in the WRNS. They tackled jobs previously considered as too delicate for women. They drove vans, rode motorbikes, were cooks, sailmakers, fitters and turners, even ships pilots. Linguists were especially welcome and worked on intelligence duties.

Scotland had its own Divisional Director based in Edinburgh and WRNS were stationed from Orkney to Galloway. A training centre for wireless telegraphists was established at Mather's Hotel in Dundee and the Royal Naval Station at Crail trained torpedo attack assessors.

Others joined the WAAF. All types of trades and services were carried out. Many women acted as plotters responsible for the safe landing of aircraft. A few were privileged to become members of the Air Transport Auxiliary which flew planes within the U.K. mainly delivering them to airfields after maintenance. Others flew as Flying Nursing Orderlies.

LOCAL GIRL IN SEARCHLIGHT UNIT

Betty Gardner [1921 -]

Our lassies are helping to bring down Nazi raiders by manning searchlight batteries. In Eastern Command in the London area is Sergeant Betty Gardner from Cellardyke. Having gained her experience in a heavy ack-ack battery she is now one of the first searchlight girls and proud of the fact that she is not merely attached to Army Command but is an actual member of the recently established Searchlight Regiment.

Her particular job is the instruction of recruits after they have passed initial training. Her most treasured possession is a letter received from a pilot thanking her for guiding him home from a raid on Hamburg.

Before volunteering for the ATS last year she was a well known and popular conductress on the East Fife Services of Messrs Alexander.

Based on an article in East Fife Observer 28th August 1943.

Dorothy Farr:

recalls volunteering for training in the RAF/ATS and attending a drill hall in Coplaw Street, Glasgow one or two evenings per week.

'We had no uniform but one Sunday we marched on parade through Glasgow wearing fashionable clothes, high heels and some of us carried umbrellas. We teetered along to ribald comments and titters from the onlookers.'

Ailsa Stevenson:

joined up in a bleak hall in Glasgow in 1939. There were two desks and by luck she arrived at the one for caterers, clerks and drivers and was offered a posting as a driver.

On Christmas Day 1939 she was one of 22 aircraftswomen feeling cold and miserable as they washed up the dishes from the airmen's mess when six officers appeared looking for a drink. One of them was Guy Gibson, later of Dambusters fame. Another was a Scot and when he realised that some of the girls were Scottish he found a piper and they had a terrific party dancing Scotch reels and so on. The girls got a bit merry on the mixture of drinks.

In 1940 in Oban not enough furniture had arrived at their base and the girls had to sleep top to tail in a single bed. During WW2 women served in the Auxiliary Territorial Service which was attached to the Army carrying out many duties similar to those in the other services. The ATS in Scotland was commanded by Miss Stirling of Gargunnock.

Bonnie Fechters ~ Women in Scotland 1900-1950

> An appeal is now being made to Scotswomen of 18+ to volunteer for national service on the land. The terms offered include board and lodgings during training, one free outfit [highboots, breeches, 2 overalls] The pay is 18/-per week [or the wages of the district, if higher]. Out of work pay at the rate of 2/6 for a period not exceeding 4 weeks.
>
> No woman to be sent to work on a farm unless conditions are approved by the Women's County Committee.
>
> As much of the work engaged in is man's work ordinarily, it is of the utmost importance that they should be of good constitution and vigorous.
>
> *Enrolment form from the Post Office, Employment Exchange or National Service Office.*

Kilsyth Chronicle 8th April 1918.

THE WOMEN'S LAND ARMY

was originally set up in 1918 at the end of WW1. It was resurrected in 1940, but was not always a popular option. It was needed because merchant ships were being torpedoed and food was scarce. Many women found the pay of 5/-per day plus keep an insult at a time when munition workers were earning £3.00 per week.

In 1942 the Women's Timber Corps was another option. Tree-felling was hard and backbreaking work and most women had never swung an axe before. They worked from 8am - 12 noon and from 12.30pm - 5pm. They lived in bothies or stable lofts with primitive facilities. Women who were conscientious objectors could choose to join this Corps.

MILITARY NURSING SERVICES

Since 1885 military nursing services had been in place, the first being the Naval Nursing Service which was followed in 1902 by the establishment of Army Nurses. In 1907 the FANY [First Aid Nursing Yeomanry] was set up. Most of the doctors and nurses came from wealthy backgrounds; it was necessary to provide your own horse.

In 1914 Queen Alexandra's Imperial Military Nursing Service, Voluntary Aid Detachments, the Territorial Force Nursing Service and the Scottish Hospitals Unit all provided volunteer medical staff in Scotland, the U.K. and to areas of need abroad.

Voluntary Aid Detachments were set up under the auspices of the Scottish Branch of the British Red Cross Society in 1914. Money was raised in Scotland to set up a 200 bed hospital in France, rest stations at the main railway stations throughout Scotland and many units in hospitals, private homes and hotels specially equipped for the purpose. One of these enjoyed an unusual setting. Springburn Red Cross Hospital was established in the Administration Building of the North British Locomotive Company. The Company paid for all structural alterations, equipment and furnishings. By 1918 there were five wards with accommodation for 400 wounded. Tiled operating theatres and an x-ray room in a former strong room were kept busy as was the staff of a Medical Superintendent, 5 assistants, Matron, 8 sisters, 17 nurses and 30 V.A.D. plus cooks, orderlies and maids. The Matron, Miss Low, was awarded the Royal Red Cross.

In a number of towns there were stores where parcels were made up to be sent out to the troops in Belgium, Serbia, France and India. The Scottish Women's Ambulance Unit provided nurses, doctors and drivers wherever help was needed at home or abroad.

'From the head of the Scottish Society to the last enrolled worker, evidence of Scottish thoroughness is in all things.'
The Way of the Red Cross 1915.

Katherine Macphail [1887-1974]:

was born in Coatbridge where her father was a G.P.. She graduated from Glasgow University in 1913 and a year later volunteered to go to Salonica with the Scottish Women's Ambulance Unit for six months. She stayed on and joined the Military Medical Unit of the Serbian Army.

In 1917 she worked in the Macedonian war area behind enemy lines until peace came when she returned to Belgrade. In 1919 she founded a hospital for children and she was superintendent from 1919 - 1933. It was eventually sold to the State and the money used to build another hospital.

This was to be the first of seven opened in 1934 with the support of Queen Marie of Yugoslavia .Known as the Anglo-Yugoslav Children's Hospital it was positioned 50 miles up the Danube from Belgrade in Kamenica. It specialised in surgical tuberculosis. Katherine stayed there until the Germans destroyed it in 1941 and she was interned by Italian forces. After her release she returned to Scotland where she worked for the Child Welfare Department of Lanarkshire County Council. Her love of Yugoslavia was such that she worked constantly in her spare time for the Relief Fund for its children. The Save the Children Fund approached her in 1944 asking her to go back to Yugoslavia to take charge of their first medical relief unit there. She was delighted to return to the hospital which she had founded. Help came in the form of grants from Save the Children, United Nations Relief and Rehabilitation Administration and the Yugoslav Government. She remained there until taking retirement in 1947 aged sixty.

Still active, she continued to work for the children she left behind. In 1954 she received the Freedom of Kamenica in recognition of the hospital's 20 years of service. She was also made Life President of the local Red Cross Society. Her decorations were many. She held the St. Sava Medal at several classes and the Serbian

Bonnie Fechters ~ Women in Scotland 1900-1950

SCOTTISH WOMEN'S HOSPITALS FOREIGN SERVICE

Dr. Elsie Inglis set up this service after an offer of help to establish units for British troops had been turned down by the Foreign Office. Funds were raised by the Scottish Federation of Women's Suffrage Societies of which she was secretary from 1906. Donations of equipment and medical supplies as well as money were received. Work parties were formed to support the units.

The first unit was offered safe transport by the Admiralty and set off for Serbia. The second unit based at the Abbaye de Royaumont near Chantilly was given to them by the French Red Cross Society. Their uniform was grey material with Gordon tartan facings.

The Service carried out a lot of essential work caring for the sick and wounded and looking after mothers and children. Many of the staff ended up behind enemy lines and became prisoners of war while others took part in the retreat of 1915, trekking with the Serbian Army over the mountains of Montenegro in atrocious wintery conditions. Several of the staff did not survive the journey.

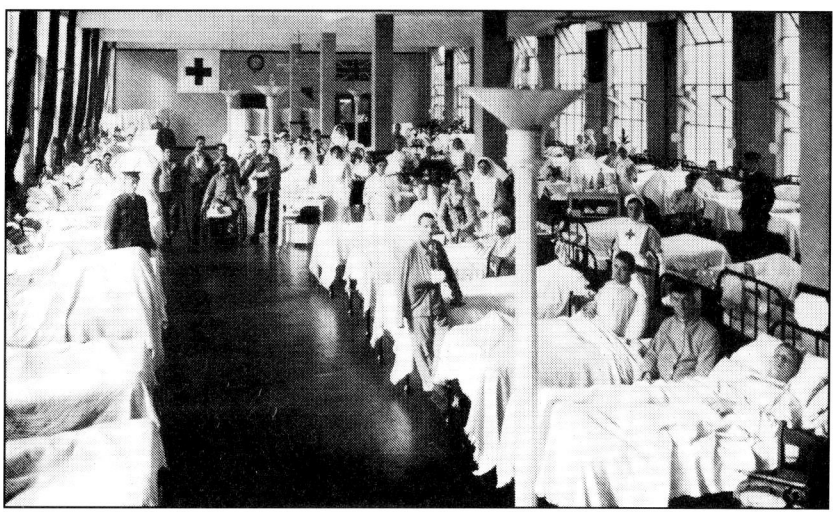

Top: Retreat from Serbia, 1915.
Bottom: Springburn Red Cross Hospital. 1914-18.

Inverclyde District Libraries
North British Locomotive Co. Ltd.

Red Cross as well as the Russian Red Cross for helping Russian children in Belgrade.

She died in St. Andrews in 1974 unaware that yet another honour had been conferred upon her. The Orthopaedic Surgeons of Yugoslavia awarded her the Order of the Yugoslav Flag with Golden Star for her work for the children of their country.

Based on a newspaper reprint in The St. Andrews Citizen 28th September 1974.

Norah Neilson Gray [1882-1931]:

was born in Helensburgh. She was an acclaimed artist who went out as a Voluntary Aid Worker to France. In her free time she produced a painting of the casualty reception area in the vaulted crypt of the Abbaye de Royaumont. She also painted the senior staff in the cloisters of the Abbey as a commission for the Women's Section of the Imperial War Museum.

Sister Jean Whyte:

of Greenock trained in the Western Infirmary, Glasgow. She came under German fire at a clearing station in Serbia.

'Gunfire started at noon and lasted for two hours. Ambulance waggons went out to rescue the wounded men returning with cases for the operating theatre. A shell exploded in the courtyard of the clearing station and the building was almost destroyed. The operating theatre received a direct hit. Several of the staff were injured and I received a few scratches. [shrapnel wounds]. The safety of the patients was uppermost in our minds and they were carried to the basement. We had to dig out our baggage from the rubble and later we were transferred with our patients to another station.'
Daily Record. 1915

Sister Whyte and three other nurses were awarded the Military Medal.

Nurse Hughes:

a district nurse in Pittenweem went to France to take up duties in a field hospital which was equipped and financed by Lady Eva Weymss of Weymss Castle whom Nurse Hughes remembers proved an able worker and interpreter.

Meta Munro Kerr [c 1895-]:

was from a comfortably off family in Lenzie. Her brothers were serving in the Forces. One a captain in the navy, one a lieutenant and the other a major in the army. Her other brother was a professor of midwifery at The Glasgow Maternity Hospital in Rottenrow, Glasgow. With her sister Jessie she volunteered as a cook with the Scottish Women's Hospital Unit and was attached to Dr. Alice Hutchison's command. She kept a diary and managed to smuggle it out. She also managed to send a letter home.

Bonnie Fechters ~ Women in Scotland 1900-1950

WW1 - THE HOME FRONT

A great deal of work was done by the women who stayed at home. The Patriotic War Work Parties were co-ordinated by district and consisted of women's guilds of every denomination which gathered together to make and distribute comforts to the troops. There was also a National Egg Collection for Wounded Soldiers to which farmers' wives contributed fresh eggs. The Soldiers and Sailors Families Association helped those widowed with rent payments and in many organisations women worked to raise funds to endow beds in hospitals at home and abroad. Although the Scottish Co-operative Women's Guild raised funds for the Disabled Soldiers and Sailors Fund it felt that it was the duty of the Government to provide for these men and their families.

Glasgow tram conductress. C1915.
Glasgow through the Looking Glass. D. Anderson

Duke and Duchess of York (later King George VI and Queen Elizabeth) with the staff of Hull Royal Infirmary. Matron Elizabeth Armstrong.

Serbia 1915
Dear Mother,
You must not be anxious about me. I am fine. I am an orderly, this is my day. Rise at 6.30a.m., dress and make breakfast for self and Miss —. Do our room and walk to hospital ten minutes away. Sweep and dust wards and corridors, sometimes scrub floors. Do odd jobs till 12.30p.m. when we return to our own room and have dinner of stew, bread, sugar and cocoa. We return to hospital to wash dirty bandages and roll clean ones, do the lamps and oddments till 4.30p.m. when we go home for tea. [bread, jam etc.] light our fire with sticks which we collect in our time off and have a good wash in a basin. Go to bed about 9p.m..
We have no books to read. Saturday is our day off when we scrub the floor and do the washing. We have two chairs, a washstand, a table and a wardrobe. There is a single bed with a wire mattress covered with folded rugs in which we sleep top to tail.
I only have my golfing hat for everything.
The Committee in Edinburgh will let you know how you should address me in writing.

In an address at a concert in Lenzie in March 1916 in aid of funds for the Scottish Hospitals she told a packed Public Hall of her experiences as a prisoner of war.

'Fighting broke out in Belgrade in October 1915 and Dr. Hutchison gathered the staff together on a Sunday morning to say that they should try to stay calm and that she would not have panic in her unit. A few days later we were told we must leave the camp.
It took four days to take down and pack tents, equipment and stores. We trekked for several days before meeting up with other units at Vranyaschka. The Serbs believed that Allied help was at hand. It was a serious situation and nurses were asked to choose whether to go or stay. Only 100 could leave. I chose to stay. Austrians entered the town and we were all taken prisoner.
Eventually after 24 hours they gave us a bowl of soup. There were three guards in the passage day and night. No one was allowed outside for three days then the guards decided to let some of us have some exercise. Ten of the fastest walkers were chosen and the guards were furious when the women walked them off their feet.
Dr. Hutchison was sent for by the Commandant who complained that he would need to find stronger men to go out with them and it was no laughing matter.
We ate black bread and were only allowed half a loaf. Washing facilities were poor. They gave us nothing but we had managed to keep a basin and saucepan of our own so we rigged up a blanket and went behind it one by one. Washing of clothes was also difficult and we would just hang them up to dry when a pack of geese or some pigs would pull them down into the mud. In towns nearby there were 300 cases of cholera. The Commandant ordered nurses to go and work with them without inoculation and with no pay. Dr. Hutchison refused and was told that as we were prisoners we had no choice. If we did not obey we would be turned out to sleep in tents and would die of cold'.

They were released in January 1916 and taken to Budapest then Vienna. Photographs were destroyed and they were all searched by women guards who were looking for gold. On 12th February 1916 they arrived at Victoria Station in London and Dr. Hutchison still carried over her arm the Union Jack which they had managed to preserve throughout their ordeal.

The streets of Lenzie were lined with people as Meta arrived by train from Glasgow. They cheered her all the way home. Her sister Jessie escaped imprisonment and ended up in Salonica.

Based on an account in the Kirkintilloch Herald 8th March 1916.

These are a sample of the accounts available in every local newspaper showing the dedicated service given by all classes of Scottish women.

Elizabeth Armstrong (above) [1873-1958]:

served as a sister with the Territorial Army Nursing Service at Dar-es-Salaam in East Africa during WW1 being awarded the Royal Red Cross in 1918. While she was there she learned to speak Swahili so that she could communicate with the native helpers. She and her three sisters had trained at Glasgow's Western Infirmary. Her elder sister, Charlotte became one of the first of Glasgow's Green Ladies, Julia was a matron in Lancashire and her youngest sister, Ellen was gassed while serving in France.

Elizabeth had been theatre sister to Sir William McEwan, the eminent surgeon, and had worked with Alexander

Bonnie Fechters ~ Women in Scotland 1900-1950

SPANISH CIVIL WAR 1936

Annie Murray [1906-] volunteered in 1936 through the British Medical Aid Association to go to help the Spanish people who were fighting fascism during the Spanish Civil War.

She trained as a nurse at Edinburgh Royal Infirmary and had been responsible while training in encouraging student nurses to protest against their conditions. The Communist ideology attracted her and she became a member of the Party.

She travelled to Spain via Perpignon in France and served in a small hospital in Huete, outside Barcelona, then later she transferred to a city hospital and became theatre nurse to Dr Quemada. It was hard and dangerous work. On one occasion they operated in the shelter of a bridge as bombs fell all around. Equipment however was fairly good. Casualties were of many different nationalities because the International Brigade was formed from volunteers from many countries. Some women fought at the Front. Hypothermia was a big threat and very painful. Annie was not fond of the food 'mainly beans and oil' and coffee 'like sand and water'.

She managed to keep in contact with her five sisters at home and her two brothers who were also fighting in Spain. She nursed in Spain for two and a half years returning to London to work in Civil Defence during the beginning of WW2. Later she worked as a matron of a nursery in Stepney. She married and after the war worked in a Post Office until she retired in 1964. She lives in Fife.

Voices from the Spanish Civil War, Ian MacDougall, Polygon, 1986.

Annie Murray (centre) and other nurses drying and folding bandages to be used again.

WW2 - THE HOME FRONT

Janet Hyslop was head warden of Group E of the Air Raid Precautions team in Clydebank. There were six groups in the Division staffed by men and women. Training started in 1938 for fire fighting and gas protection.

'I used to feel terrible, me, a young woman, telling men in the factories how to fight fires. We had to organise teams to guide people into shelters if there was an emergency. We learned the hard way as we had only a vague idea of what might be needed. I visited Coventry and saw the devastation and casualties there.

I had a premonition that night [13th March 1941] that there was something up in the sky that was menacing. The Blitz when it came at 9p.m. wiped out all essential services and set fire to a wide area. It went on and on and I remember someone shouting up 'Hiv ye nae hame tae go tae.'

The First Aid Post got a direct hit. There were 60 casualties taken to the church hall with broken limbs, scratches and shattered faces. Between two and three p.m. I spoke to a young woman who arrived thinking it was a First Aid Post. She went away disappointed. About 5a.m. several white coated men

---

Fleming before penicillin was discovered. She never married as her fiance, who was a doctor, was posted missing at sea. She served also as Matron of Hull Royal Infirmary from 1923 until 1938 when she retired to look after her brother who was now blind.

Every year on Armistice Day until her death in 1958, the sitting room mantelpiece was draped with miniature Union Jacks and Lion Rampant flags; photographs and medals were put on display; the bronze plaque commemorating her sister Ellen's death took pride of place. In 1953 she was thrilled to be able to see the ceremony of Remembrance at the cenotaph in Whitehall for the first time on television.

Personal interview, Springboig, 1955.

WW2. Peebles Hydro was requisitioned on the 4th September 1939 and troops decanted from a train which stopped on the railway line bordering the grounds. Orders were given to strip the Hydro of its finery which was then stored away. All the carpets were lifted and the ballroom floor treated to avoid slipping. It was filled with 1200 hospital beds for the 23rd [Scottish] General Hospital T.A.. The operating theatre was housed in the Bridal Suite. The nursing sisters' quarters were in the attics and their mess was in a basement at the back of the hotel. Meanwhile the male officers swanned it in The Bruce Lounge, complete with billiard table.

Millie Bell:

It was cold at night, cheerless and grim especially up in the attics where we were billeted. To add some warmth and sparkle to our lot we gathered fir cones in our kit bags from the wood behind and kindled a good fire in a different room each night. The difficulty was in getting the fuel up in the lift without coming face to face with the colonel- a holy terror. The flowers had been dug out of the plots at the front entrance and replaced with parsley which we used as a filling for our breakfast rolls along with our daily butter ration which was the size of half a crown. It was supposed to give us zest.

The Queen Alexandra's Nursing Sisters wore a grey cotton frock with a shoulder cape trimmed with scarlet and on their heads a veil of fine starched lawn.

Other women drove a fleet of Red Cross ambulances some, being American vehicles, had a left hand drive.

The Story of Peebles Hydro, Heather Thom, 1987.

Bonnie Fechters ~ Women in Scotland 1900-1950

arrived. They were a team of doctors from the Western Infirmary. That lassie had made her way there and told them 'They can't come to you. You'll need to go to them.'

I remember that everywhere you looked there were women wearing fur coats and clasping the few precious possessions which they had salvaged. The men had on their best suits and bowler hats.

There was excitement but no panic. People just coped. Buses were to be laid on to take people away to safety in Cumbernauld, Kirkintilloch, East Kilbride and the Loch Lomond area. The folks didn't know where they were going. It was a long night. At last about 6a.m. the all-clear sounded. The next night there were mainly Civil Defence people in the town. Everyone who could go had been evacuated. Nearly all the houses were damaged. The soldiers were brought in to prevent looting and I had to detail them what needed looking after. A group of miners came from Fife. They helped to unearth the remains of furniture etc.. They knew the right technique. We just pulled at anything we saw which simply made things worse'.

Step/CDC Project Tape, Education Resource Service, Dunbarton Division 1981.

Help from Edinburgh: Women's Canteen Work

The homeless people in the Clydebank area are now receiving the benefit of Edinburgh's W.V.S. Centre which has been working overtime since the raiders' visit to the West, turning out 'waggon loads' of clothing from the American Red Cross.

Lady Ruth Balfour, chairman, has paid a personal visit to the bombed area and has allocated members of her staff to relieve the existing services. Two mobile canteens which arrived at a West of Scotland dock from the American Red Cross have been set up in Clydeside where they are doing grand work in feeding the homeless.

Daily Express report March 1941.

WOMEN'S VOLUNTARY SERVICE

The Women's Voluntary Service for Air Raid Precautions was formed in the early summer of 1938. Its purpose was to awaken the women of Britain to the danger which threatened from air attack and to encourage them to come to the aid of their country. The Home Secretary invited the Dowager Marchioness of Reading to form, under the auspices of the Government, a nationwide organisation which would assist local authorities everywhere with the work of recruiting and training women to serve what were then known as the Air Raid Precautions Services.

Civil Defence was its first priority but this soon expanded to cover a wide variety of voluntary work. Evacuation of children was the first major undertaking and the women of the W.V.S. helped in their transportation, finding of billets and settling them into their new homes. The Housewives Section helped the A.R.P. and the public during and after raids and the W.V.S. ran Incident Inquiry Posts where people could find out about their relatives.

Mobile canteens provided food and hot drinks for those experiencing a raid and the women learned how to cook amongst the debris of an air raid. They managed to produce around 4000 hot meals during and after the Clydebank Blitz. They also ran Rest Centres.

Clothing was issued to those who had lost everything and clothing exchanges were also run to help make the most of what was available. The W.V.S. helped to distribute ration books to every home in Scotland within a week. They helped to set up and run British Restaurants. Mass cooking and feeding made the best use of scarce resources. They also operated the School Meals Service and members took meat pies to those working on the land under the Agricultural Pie Scheme. They set up a Volunteer Car Pool, acted as station guides and organised station canteens for servicemen. They collected rosehips and herbs and made jam, collected vegetables to feed men on minesweepers and staffed servicemen's clubs.

At the end of the War it was decided to continue this service which used the time and talents of thousands of women. The W.V.S. received the accolade of having 'Royal' added into its title. Today in towns throughout Scotland it carries out duties of great benefit to the community including canteens for visitors in hospitals and prisons. The Meals on Wheels Scheme which takes hot meals to the elderly housebound began in Scotland in 1947.

In 1950, a Mrs. Craig visited wards in Stobhill Hospital, Glasgow with a large basket filled with sweets. It was such a popular service that the ladies of the Bishopbriggs Branch of the W.R.V.S. upgraded it to a trolley and have continued this much appreciated access to newspapers, confectionery and toiletries. They also run a shop while Lenzie W.R.V.S. are responsible for the tearoom.

From Stobhill, the First Seventy Years by O.M.Watt. Robert Maclehose, 1971.

WVS organising evacuation at the beginning of WW2. Railways in Wartime, E.F. Carter.

WOMEN'S PARLIAMENT

156 delegates from 97 organisations met in Glasgow on Burns Night 25th January 1940 and passed a Bill to ensure the effective use of women power in the defence of the country. They demanded communal feeding centres, nurseries with trained staff, medical facilities, full-time education, school meals, play centres, better working hours, equal pay and regular training for women workers. Skilled women were to be encouraged to use their skills and not be placed in mundane jobs.

Women were mobilised in every sense of the word and from the 1950s married women began to work in ever increasing numbers as more and better household gadgets were introduced. By the 1960s freezers and convenience foods had taken over along with supermarkets and it was no longer necessary to shop every day leaving them freer to study or work.

Bonnie Fechters ~ Women in Scotland 1900-1950

Sweaty Socks & Herb Wives

Faith, Hope and Charity.

In the first half of the 20th century Scottish women did not expect to have good health. Often they were worn out from childbearing or suffering from a poor diet and damp housing conditions. They had to be really ill to seek medical help. 'You waited till you realised that something was really wrong,' was how one woman put it.

There was a tendency to put others before themselves. Many had large families and also coped with their own or their husband's parents and single relatives. Often by forty they were worn out by sheer hard work.

Women were usually considered to be knowledgeable about health matters and both good and bad ideas about home cures and herbal medicines were handed down from one generation to the next. Herb wives, howdies and spaewives were all better thought of than any doctor.

To visit a doctor or have one come to the house cost money and unless the situation was serious attempts were made to deal with illness at home. Wage earners were insured under the National Insurance Act of 1911. Sickness benefit covered free treatment and medicines and a weekly payment but did not extend to the family, only the insured person. Hospital treament was not included in the scheme but those hospitals maintained by charities gave treatment free to anyone unable to pay and, through lines issued by subscribers, to many others.

'My mother was regularly 'consulted' by neighbours as to how to treat themselves and their families, especially the children. I hated one of her favourite cures for a sore throat. She wrapped a heated, sweaty sock round my neck. I believe the idea was that the oil from the wool and the warmth would soothe it but why it needed to smell I don't know. To avoid colds a bag of camphor was hung around your neck. I suppose inhaling it kept the tubes open. For whooping cough it was the same idea. The patient should be taken to where someone was working with hot tar. Poultices for boils or a chest infection were made. A bread poultice was a favourite or hot salt in a muslin bag. Posh folk bought tins of kaolin which was a bit like cement. It was heated and spread onto a cloth then slapped onto your chest. It was not very pleasant and lumpy when it had cooled.'

Margaret Peters, personal interview, Abbeyfield, Lenzie, 1986.

PATENT MEDICINES

blatantly targeted women in newspaper and magazine advertisements. These miracle cures seemed to be effective for every and any complaint. Pills, potions and elixirs made names like Beechams a household word. Adverts appeared in the classified section such as those for Mrs Ellis's Pills for Females, 2/9 or extra strong 4/9 and Widow Welch's Female Pills 1/3 or 3/-. The latter coming with a testimonial. It won a Certificate of Merit at the Tasmanian Exhibition, 1881 and promised instant relief for all sorts of troubles.

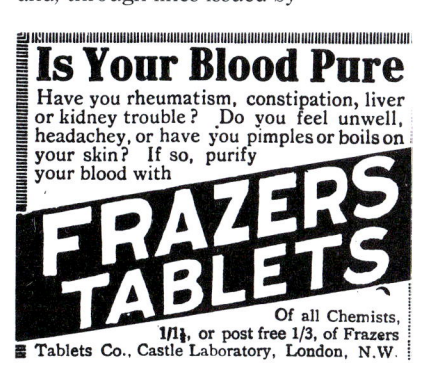

Bonnie Fechters ~ Women in Scotland 1900-1950

Tonic wines made from herbal recipes were also popular, especially with those who were in favour of temperance. Sanatogen and Wincarnis were recommended as a cure for anaemia which did affect many women whose diet was lacking in iron. Another favourite was chemical food, a bitter tasting potion made up in doctors' dispensaries or by pharmacists. The red colouring of all of these concoctions as well as beetroot was considered as capable of replenishing the blood. Ironically money spent on self medication probably cost as much or more than a visit to the doctor.

In rural areas it would be very difficult for women to reach a doctor or attend a hospital. Many relied on herbal cures. Knowing the powers of each plant and which illness it would cure was a craft handed down through the generations. The uses of roots and plants varied. They could be boiled with alcohol to produce tinctures, have boiling water poured over leaves to produce infusions or have roots or bark steeped to provide decoctions. Others were pounded into ointments or used for poultices. Misuse could prove fatal if an overdose was administered. Herbs were often grown in large houses in the physic garden specifically for their healing powers. Plants could also be used for beauty treatment. Women who had this knowledge were revered almost like the witch doctors in the tropics.

The well-off visited spas or hydropathics. There were many built on the Clyde coast and others in the countryside in Perthshire and the Borders. There was a spa at Strathpeffer. The regime was strict in these temperance hotels with lights put out at 10.30p.m.. In these establishments water treatments were scientifically carried out and included Turkish baths and mud baths as well as massage and a form of aromatherapy. There was also a variety of electrical therapy treatments.

Doctors often carried out operations in the patient's own home.

Nurses, North Uist, Inverness-shire. National Museums of Scotland

'I remember my daughter having her tonsils and adenoids taken out at home on the dining-room table. This was quite common. The doctor arrived with an anaesthetist to administer chloroform by putting a mask over her face. There was only water boiled in the kettle for the instruments and no special lights or anything. I think I paid 7/6. This would be about 1944.'

Margaret Peters, personal interview, Abbeyfield, Lenzie, 1986.

Some doctors charged their well-off patients and gave free treatment where they saw the necessity.

'That'll be a shilling if you have it - if you haven't, it can lie over.'

Dr. Craig, the 'poorman's' doctor in Mrs. Barry, a novel by Frederick Niven is typical. He also ran a free clinic but the patients had to agree to be examined by students. This was based on the Glasgow Medical Mission in Gorbals.

CHILDBIRTH

was a mystery to many women of all classes. It was something rarely discussed in better class homes and easily misunderstood. Most women, unless they had been nurses, were ignorant of the mechanics. Anatomy and physiology were not taught at school. Ideas were gleaned from their mothers and from friends and neighbours but often this was:
'Oh, it's your first,' a response which might lead to horror stories about themselves and others until the poor mother-to-be was in a complete panic.

'You went to the doctor who poked around a wee bit and listened to your tummy and I asked him if he had to cut it open to get the baby out'

was what one woman respondent recalled in an oral interview for the Stirling Women's Oral History Project, 1988.

Any form of anaesthesia used to alleviate the pain of childbirth was considered by some people as against the will of God and the idea that pain was the gift of Providence, which would make mothers more appreciative of their baby, was held by many including some doctors and nurses. Some women sewed their shroud and put it away with the baby clothes which were awaiting the new arrival such was the uncertainty of them surviving the birth process.

Some women went into a maternity hospital. Those hospitals which admitted women whose babies were illegitimate were often criticised by the self righteous. Some women went into private nursing homes run by midwives for profit or to fee-paying hospitals such as Redlands in Glasgow's west end. Other midwives would take in one or two women to their own homes for a fee but the majority of babies were born at home.

Fathers were rarely present at the birth of their babies until the late 1960s. Birth was women's business. Neighbours helped out and would prepare food for the other children and the husband who might not even be able to boil an egg. The local howdie as those who regularly assisted at births were known would put her life experience at the mother's service.

After the passing of the Midwives Act in 1915, however, all women attending a birth had to have undergone training before being allowed to practise. Registration of midwives was also introduced. Nevertheless if the howdie had been successfully practising for some time before the Act she would be accepted onto the register. After 1916 there were local authority midwives who could be called in. A doctor usually only attended if complications appeared. After 1922 only qualified midwives were permitted to conduct a birth. Women were kept in bed for up to two weeks. Many suffered from puerperal or childbed fever. The percentage of deaths of the mother from puerperal fever, per 1000 births remaining steady at 2.5 over a long period. After the introduction of the Midwives Act more cases came to light. About 6 per 1000 in 1911, 7 per 1000 in 1916 and 10 per 1000 in 1921. The death toll however fell. Another problem was white leg which was caused by a lack of circulation and resolved when the practice of laying-in was abandoned and women were encouraged to get up and about as soon as possible.

Support for mothers with babies and other children developed slowly despite the obvious and pressing need for health care.

In 1900 the infant mortality rate in Glasgow was 140 per 1000 live births. By 1921 this had fallen to 107. The first woman medical officer was appointed in Glasgow in 1906. The Glasgow Infant Health Visitors Association provided voluntary visitors. These were usually middle-class women with a social conscience, who held classes for expectant mothers in homecraft, including making a drawer into a cradle, converting towels into bath aprons and sewing flannelette gowns for babies. This organisation was set up by the Charity Organisation Society and the British Women's Temperance Association's Scottish Branch. They divided the city into 19 wards with around 300 voluntary visitors who went into the homes with new babies and offered advice on feeding, hygiene and clothing.

In 1907 the Notification of Births Act was passed and in 1908 adopted by the Corporation of Glasgow which appointed its first Green Lady, as the health visitors came to be known because of their distinctive uniform of green coat and hat. Two more were appointed in 1910 and two lady doctors and seven more health visitors followed in 1915 with the adoption of the Midwives Act. In 1916, Kirkintilloch decided to advertise the post of Health Visitor at £80 per year plus uniform but she also had to be competent to discharge the duties of assistant sanitary inspector.

A higher rate of stillbirths was reported to mothers employed in factories than to non-working mothers. The statistics also show, unsurprisingly, that stillbirths were lower in better class residential districts. Infant clinics, children's homes, country homes and Fresh Air Fortnights at places like Ardgoil on the shores of Loch Goil offered mothers and children a break from city life. Girl Guide officers often volunteered to staff these holiday homes. Since 1883 the Day Nurseries Association had provided nurseries and creches for mothers who had to work away from home. The Association also ran the Cosy Corner Restaurant with an area set aside for expectant and nursing mothers who paid 3d for a meal. Under the Child Welfare Scheme from 1910 classes in cookery and sewing were held during winter months. Maternity bundles supplied by working parties from churches' Dorcas, Zenana and other clothing societies were distributed and the Poor Children's Clothing Guild served older children in the same way. Many towns had clothing societies staffed voluntarily by local women.

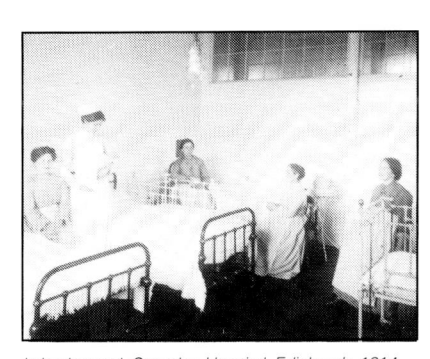

Lying-in ward, Greenlee Hospital, Edinburgh, 1914. Lothian Regional Council, Social Work Dept.

BIRTH CONTROL

'It wasn't how many you wanted. It was how many you got'

Until the arrival of the contraceptive pill in the 1960s women had a limited choice in preventing unwanted pregnancy. Most had a vague notion that 'rubber goods' or special sponges existed but had not investigated further. Many men would have been horrified at the thought of limiting their family. The Birth Control League was active in the Fife coalfields in 1918. Women flocked to hear Margaret Sanger, an American, when she spoke about birth control at Glasgow Green in 1920 but opposition came from strange bedfellows. Both the Roman Catholic Church and the Marxists were opposed not only for moral reasons but also from a fear of limiting the number of their own supporters. The Church of Scotland remained silent on the issue. There were only 20 voluntary birth control clinics in Scotland until 1930. Members of the Scottish Co-operative Women's Guild helped to spread information by speaking at meetings and encouraging the publication of leaflets which could be distributed at clinics.

Another problem which affected women's health was venereal disease brought home to them by men from the forces serving abroad or caught through a life of prostitution. There had been for more than half a century clinics and hospitals which treated these diseases but as the number of cases grew after WW1 more attention was paid to the treatment of women and children who had been infected. Dr. Nora Wattie came to Glasgow in 1924 to specialise in this treatment and it was a source of delight for her to achieve a complete cure in a growing number of cases, especially when new born babies could be saved from blindness.

HOSPITALS

Until the National Health Act 1948 when all hospitals were nationalised funds had to be found to keep them running. The District Nursing Association was active in most towns and volunteers collected regularly from each subscriber. They also ran fund raising fetes and dances. In Kirkintilloch they ran an annual festival week called Rob Royal, the name of a local football team being Rob Roy. Concerts, competitions, fancy dress parades, cruises, dances and a fete were organised in aid of Glasgow Royal Infirmary.

Voluntary Hospitals had been set up in the 18th century by subscriptions from individuals, friendly societies and workplaces. These were usually the large infirmaries and teaching hospitals in Scotland's cities. They were run by a board of governors. They generally dealt only with acute illnesses. Public hospitals were run by the local authority in conjunction with the Poor Law until 1930. Only then was the stigma of the Poorhouse removed and the name of general hospital adopted. Many of the infectious diseases hospitals came into this category.

State and private asylums were usually large stone mansions in their own grounds and inmates were openly referred to as feeble-minded, imbeciles or cretins. Some hospitals specialised in catering for women, others cared for children or the young incurables and in the country sanatoria were built for the treatment of tuberculosis.

Convalescent homes were often built and equipped by trade unions, friendly societies, specific industries [e.g. railways], by public subscription and occasionally were privately owned and run for profit. They gave patients a chance to recuperate after an operation or illness usually beside the sea or in the country. All these institutions employed staff and brought employment, often to non-industrial areas. Sometimes there was not enough money raised through charitable giving to make a project viable and it folded. This was the case at the convalescent home which was established at Garscube by the Glasgow Maternity Hospital and it had to close its doors in 1923.

DOCTORS

Women had a hard fight to become accepted as doctors and even after qualifying could not always find a post. The first was an English woman Dr. Sophia Jex-Blake [1840-1912] who with six others attended classes at Edinburgh. She was not allowed to graduate there and had to do so in Dublin.

Women doctors sometimes married their male colleagues and set up in joint practice. The husband was referred to as Doctor, his spouse either as Dr. Jean, or whatever her Christian name was, or 'The wife'. While some women patients preferred women doctors others did not trust them and did not think that they could be competent. Women rarely qualified as surgeons and even today relatively few consultants are women. Women doctors were expected to cover the less prestigious areas of surgery and were often given only temporary appointments. It was 1943 before the first woman doctor was appointed to the staff of the Western Infirmary in Glasgow.

Marion Gilchrist [1863 -1952]:

A pupil of Hamilton Academy she was the first woman to graduate in Scotland Mb,CM in 1894 from Queen Margaret College of Glasgow University. She specialised in opthalmology and worked at the Victoria Infirmary from 1914 until 1930. This infirmary was not held in great esteem by the men in the profession and it was easier for women to find a post there. She was active in the Glasgow Branch of the British Medical Association and was its first woman chairman. She also was involved with the Medical Women's Federation and the Muirhead Trust which supported medical education for girls. She was also a suffragist, initially in the Women's Social and Political Union, latterly in the breakaway Women's Freedom League and was Surgeon-in-Chief in Scottish Women's Hospitals Foreign Service.

Elsie Maud Inglis (above) [1864 - 1917]:

was born in India and came to Edinburgh in 1878 qualifying as a doctor in 1892. She applied unsuccessfully for the position of House Surgeon at the Glasgow Maternity Hospital when John Munro Kerr was appointed. While working at the Elizabeth Garrett Anderson Hospital in London she became interested in the campaign for women's suffrage. She returned to Edinburgh in 1894 and graduated as a surgeon in 1899. She set up a hospice for women and children from slum areas. In 1901 she set up a hospital which specialised in surgery for women and which was staffed entirely by women.

In 1906, Elsie Inglis was appointed secretary of the Scottish Federation of Women's Suffrage Societies of which she was a founder member and spoke at meetings throughout Scotland. Her work with working-class women gave her an understanding of their needs and she was a tireless worker on their behalf. In 1914 she founded the Scottish Women's Hospital Unit for Foreign Service with support both practical and financial from the S.F.W.S.S.. She served in Serbia, Rumania and Russia. Under duress she managed to send two of her staff to Britain with a message of 2500 words which they learned by heart. She died at the age of 53, three days after returning to Scotland in 1917.

In the 1920's the Elsie Inglis Maternity Hospital was opened in Edinburgh to honour this pioneer of women's medicine.

Miss Helen Lowe was honorary treasurer of the hospital when it was handed over to the NHS in 1948. Now 90 years of age and still a practising accountant in Edinburgh she is taking part in a new fight to save the demolition of the now closed hospital preferring an option that it be retained for community use. In 1957 she was one of ten women who forced the Scottish Secretary of State to reconsider when a proposal was made to staff the hospital with male consultants.

Anne Louise McIlroy [1878 - 1968]:

graduated as a doctor in 1899 from Glasgow University and after further study she became a gynaecological surgeon at the Victoria Infirmary from 1906 - 1910. She then served as the Outdoor House Surgeon for the West End Branch of the Glasgow Maternity Hospital

Bonnie Fechters ~ Women in Scotland 1900-1950

NURSES

paid for their training and supplied their own uniforms. They had to live in the Nurses' Home and board and lodging was deducted from their meagre pay. At the beginning of the century life was very tough for probationers and they must have wanted desperately to become nurses to accept the conditions imposed on them. They worked a 12 hour day beginning at 4a.m. with an early breakfast, then on the ward until 6.30a.m. when a second breakfast was provided. Dinner was eaten at 1.15p.m. and they returned to the ward until 4.45p.m.. They were free until supper at 6.45p.m. and had to be in bed by 7.30p.m.. They also had to study for examinations in their free time. In 1916 conditions had improved and although they received no salary for the first three months they then earned £10 per year in the first year, £15 in second year and £20 in their third. The day began for student nurses at 7.30 a.m. until 8p.m. with two breaks totalling two hours for dinner and tea. They had one whole day off per month.

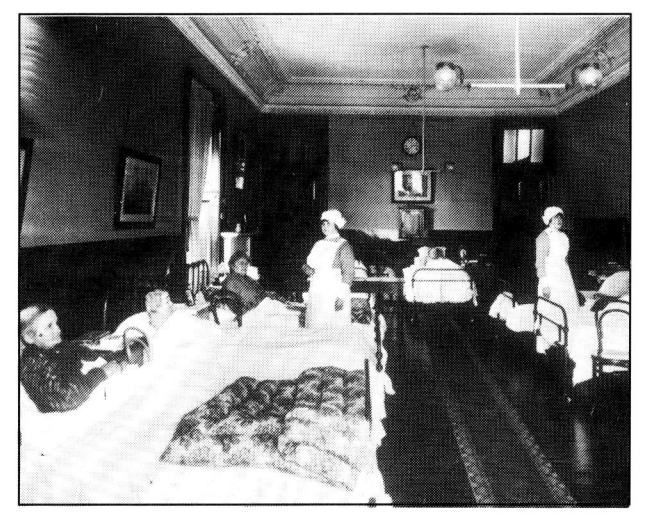

Students had to clean out and boil the metal mugs used for sputum by T.B. patients and tend to the gaping bed sores of the elderly patients who in those days were confined to bed at all times. They also had to empty and sterilise bedpans. The assistant matron of Stobhill in 1903 received £60 per year while the barber earned £67 and the porter £65. Nursing has always been seen as a vocation and has been monetarily undervalued.

Broomhill Home, women's ward. c1925   Strathkelvin District Libraries

being responsible for attending home births especially if there were complications. She resigned in 1913. During WW1 she was in command of a unit of the Scottish Women's Hospital, first in France then in Salonica. She established a School of Nursing for Serbian girls. Several honours were awarded to her including the Order of St. Sava from Serbia and the Croix de Guerre avec Palme from France. In 1921, aged 54, she became the first woman professor of Obstetrics and Gynaecology at London University. She was a founder fellow of the Royal College of Obstetricians and Gynaecologists. She practised in Harley Street. She was awarded the accolade of Dame of the British Empire in 1929 and was elected a Fellow of the Royal College of Physicians in 1937. During WW2, after her official retirement, she organised emergency midwifery services in Buckinghamshire.

Margaret Fairlie (above) [1891 - 1963]:

became at the age of 49, the first woman professor to hold the chair of midwifery at St. Andrews University from 1940 -1956. Born in Arbroath in 1891 she graduated MB,ChB from St. Andrews in 1915. After working in Dundee, Perth and Edinburgh she took up a post at St. Mary's, Manchester where she specialised in obstetrics, gynaecology and midwifery. In 1919, she returned to Scotland, working at Dundee Royal Infirmary and also consulting privately. She was visiting gynaecologist to all the hospitals in Angus and North Fife.

In 1922 she qualified as a surgeon and became a pioneer in the use of radium in the treatment of cancer. She introduced it into her work in 1926 after a visit to the Marie Curie Foundation in Paris. During WW2 all radium in Scotland was commandeered as a safeguard against bombing and her supplies were buried deep in the Sidlaw Hills.

In 1936 she was made a Fellow of the Royal College of Obstetricians and Gynaecologists and in 1957 she received an honorary degree of Doctor of Law from St. Andrews University. On her retiral, after 31 years at Dundee, she became Consultant Emeritus in Obstetrics, the first woman in Scotland to gain this honour.

In her obituary notice in The Citizen, 20th July 1963, Professor Patrick of St. Andrews is quoted as saying,

'Her relations with her students were friendly and she was highly esteemed for her teaching. No male professor had a better control of a class.'

Rebecca Strong (above) [1843-1944]:

was born in London and married young. She was widowed in her early twenties and was left with a son to support. Through a friend she

Bonnie Fechters ~ Women in Scotland 1900-1950

THE LADIES AUXILIARY

was an organisation started up to provide hospital patients with 'comforts'. Through them wirelesses and, later, televisions were supplied. Presents at Christmas, and treats throughout the year came from the money raised by these groups. They also visited and took an interest in patients who had no friends or relatives nearby.

The introduction of the National Health Service in Scotland in July 1948 gradually created a change of attitude to health care. Women began to visit the dentist: a high proportion of Scottish women needed artificial teeth owing to years of neglect. More women now wore spectacles which at first were supplied free, without any means test, under the new scheme.

There was a choice of occupations connected with medicine which appealed to women. Almoners, dieticians, physiotherapists, radiographers and administrators were considered suitable careers.

Mount Blow Children's Home, for children suffering from rickets and Malnutrition   Clydebank District Libraries

Although the Glasgow Royal Maternity Hospital set up a scheme for donation of blood in 1936 the Blood Transfusion Service as it is today developed after 1948. Many women members of the Voluntary Aid Detachments which were disbanded in 1947, took part in the establishment of blood banks and in the running of the Blood Transfusion Service's mobile units.

---

was accepted for training at the Nightingale School for Nurses at St. Thomas's Hospital in London. During this time she gained experience in a variety of hospitals. In one she was reprimanded for taking a patient's temperature, with a thermometer two feet long and shaped like a shepherd's crook, the first nurse ever to do so. She performed the task accurately and was allowed to go on doing it. On another occasion she was reported for refusing to drink the beer which was provided for the nurses but she believed that all hospital staff should support temperance. In 1876 she applied for and was appointed as Matron of Dundee Royal Infirmary.

She was appalled at the lack of training and began practical lessons on the wards. In 1879 she became Matron of Glasgow Royal Infirmary where the standard of nursing was even lower than at Dundee. She decided that ward training needed to be supplemented by classes but these still had to be taken in the nurses' free time.

'It was weary work; sleepy, tired nurses trying to take an interest in what they knew would be useful to them, and we unable to give them leisure',

she recalled in an interview in the Glasgow Herald on the occasion of her 96th birthday in August 1939.

She approached the Board of the Royal about building a nurses' home and resigned in protest when this idea was turned down. In 1885 she opened a private nursing home with the backing of the eminent surgeon Sir William McEwan. When a vacancy occurred in 1891 she was invited to apply for re-instatement in her former position as Matron at Glasgow Royal Infirmary which by this time had established a home for its nurses.

She set up a preliminary training school at which every student nurse had to undergo a course of theory and practice before being allowed to work on the wards. Pupils paid 2 guineas and provided their own board and lodgings for three months during which time they had lessons in medical theory, nursing and cookery. She gradually designed a course which led to State Registration of nurses in 1893 and her methods set the standard for nursing qualifications world-wide.

She also designed a uniform for her nurses, a dress of striped cotton fabric in deep blue with a stiff white apron. She sewed some of the first outfits herself.

She retired from nursing in 1907 at the age of 65 but served on the International Council of Nurses and attended conferences on nursing at home and abroad until she was 86 years of age. On her 96th birthday she was awarded the O.B.E. at a special ceremony held in the Glasgow Royal Infirmary where she spoke to young nurses urging them to 'preserve their faith in the essential nobility of their work' and on her 100th birthday in 1943 in the course of an interview said,

'A great many people thought that I was conceited over my work. They little know. Nobody was more fully conscious than I that I was only a pioneer and the work I did could mean nothing at all today except for the way in which it has grown and developed.'

Her relaxation was Alpine climbing and she travelled the world broadcasting. She founded the Glasgow Nurses Club and was described by one of her grandchildren on her 100th birthday as 'having a mind untrammelled by prejudice'. She died peacefully in 1944 still interested in the welfare of 'her' nurses.

Bonnie Fechters ~ Women in Scotland 1900-1950

PHILANTHROPISTS

Women who had plenty of money sometimes chose to use their wealth for the good of humanity. They are now thought of sneeringly as 'do-gooders' but these women, usually daughters of businessmen and often single, gave vast sums to the community instead of living in luxury because they held strong principles. Most were deeply committed Christians who felt it was their duty to attempt to alleviate suffering when they could. Many of them were also confirmed abstainers from alcohol and tried to save souls from the demon drink. There were a number of women who tried hard to alleviate the problems of those caught in the web of poverty.

Lady Weir supported the Fresh Air Fortnight Scheme by furnishing and equipping a home at Callander. Kate Cranston of tearoom fame took out insurance for her staff to cover medical fees. She also supported orphans and single mothers. Mrs Thomson, the wife of a stockbroker, bought up property for the use of elderly domestic servants who had no home of their own. The Salvation Army was also active in these spheres.

SOCIAL WORK

was carried on by all the above organisations and by other agencies. The churches of all denominations were involved in this as was the Salvation Army. Their familiar navy blue uniforms plus the bonnet with its red ribbon were a familiar sight. These women braved the dens of iniquity, selling the War Cry newspaper and collecting in public houses for their cause. Another familiar sight were the Sisters of Charity with their stiff white bonnets which were turned up at the edges and their black gowns, as were the Sisters of Mercy who collected for the work of the St. Vincent de Paul Society.

There were many missions run by women. The Women's Own Tent Mission, the Railway Mission, the Bethesda Mission, the Legion of Mary and many more. These along with the 'slum sisters' of the Salvation Army worked with the down and outs. Homes for unmarried mothers, accommodation for single working girls and convalescent homes were provided and maintained by charity. The Women's Help Society and the National Vigilance Society also ran homes. The Abstainers Union built the large Kilmun Convalescent Home on the shores of the Holy Loch and the Co-operative Society had several homes throughout Scotland. Although much of the work was voluntary, at such homes there was also a paid staff which gave work to many women.

The University Settlements were run by women students and provided nurseries and girls' clubs. They also ran charity shops. Mrs. Curr in Dundee left money for the Children's Free Breakfast and City Mission which also held Saturday night Gospel concerts. Jessie Craig of Craig's Tearooms in Glasgow ensured that all left-over teabread went to the needy.

While there were many women willing to do their bit there were others who used charity work as a social accessory. Many were hypocrites who patronised the poor. Others were always willing to work for causes in countries far away but did not want to face the problems on their own doorstep.

Catherine Forrester-Paton (above) [1854-1914]:

was born in Alloa and educated at Alloa Academy and in Edinburgh. She could have lived a comfortable life, travelled the world and enjoyed life at her leisure but instead she chose to follow her interests in the welfare of others and to work to make life better for others.

She founded the local branch of the British Women's Temperance Association which had an eventual membership of around 2000 women. It was more than a gathering of those who wanted to save others from the evils of drink. This branch acted as a District Nursing Association and provided two District Nurses, one for Sauchie, the other for Alloa. It also paid for their upkeep. Catherine was appointed president of the Scottish Branch of the BWTA.

At her own expense she built and equipped the County Accident Hospital, serving on the first Board. She worked for the Alloa Ladies Benevolent Society, the Day Home, the Blind Society and the Bible Society. She was president of the Women's Missionary Society and founder and chief director of the Burnbank Missionary Training Home which sent over 200 young women of all denominations into missionary service. She kept in touch with many of them at their posts abroad by letter. She was president of the local Young Women's Christian Association and of the Girls Auxiliary of the Women's Missionary Society. She also gave money to Quarriers Homes for Orphans, Bridge of Weir and the City Infirmaries.

There were representatives of many organisations at her funeral and, it is interesting to note, many women were amongst them. Mrs Milne, the vice-president of the BWTA (Scotland), and another woman were pall-bearers. It was unusual even in 1950 for women to attend funerals especially at the graveside.

Based on reports in Alloa Advertiser 15th August 1914.

Bonnie Fechters ~ Women in Scotland 1900-1950

TEMPERANCE

spawned a range of societies. The International Order of Good Templars had women in its branches but it was their work with the Little White Ribboners in which they excelled. Membership of this was open to children aged from 1 month to 7 years. It was a case of get them young and the message will stick. They also ran the Band of Hope for older children. The IOGT had lodges with names like the Anchor of Hope and the members were referred to as brother or sister.

The Abstainers Union, The Women's Temperance League and the Catholic League of the Cross all had women members as did the Order of Rechabites which called its meeting place a tent. The Rechabites had to sign a pledge ' no strong drink shall ever pass my lips', this even included sherry in a trifle. Other organisations campaigned against spirits but were less strict about wine or beer. Prohibition was not supported by all societies and the issue created friction within the broad temperance movement.

The British Women's Temperance Association [Scottish Branch] was the largest association in Scotland. Women were attracted to it because it gave them an opportunity to be of service. Its aim was to save their sisters' souls from eternal damnation and to assist those whose husbands were feckless and spent their money on drink, leaving wives and families without enough money to live on.

The father of Mary Slessor was unable to hold down a job because of drink. The family moved from Aberdeen to Dundee so that Mary's mother, a weaver, could earn enough money to keep them. Drink was seen as the greatest social evil at that time. The simplistic answer of the prohibition movement was to ban the sale of alcohol. There was, however, little attempt to understand or investigate the reason why so many men and women had recourse to it, often as an escape from a humdrum life and poverty. In many families in times of stress it was the men who turned to alcohol while their wives mainly turned to charity work and the church.

Temperance organisations often held lantern slide shows and concerts on a Saturday night where tea and cakes were served. These were well attended. The subject of the show was nearly always harrowing, being full of pictures of women in shawls, ragged children crouched outside a public house waiting for their parents to come out and evictions. The concerts were welcomed and many women were included in the galaxy of local singers who regaled the gathering with well known Victorian ballads and Scottish songs. Others were in demand as pianists.

"Poor kiddies! they're waiting for their father and mother. We working-class girls can't do much to help them now Jenny — but wait till we get the vote!"   Coracle

---

Mary Lily Walker [1863 -1918]:

was an early social worker who attended classes in Dundee at a college founded by Mary Ann Baxter of the mill-owning family. She went to London to work at the Women's University Settlement in Southwark where one of her colleagues was Octavia Hill. She then served with the Order of The Grey Ladies before returning to Dundee to work for the Social Union where she organised a Burial Society which had 10,000 women members. She bought a house which became Grey Lodge, a non-denominational settlement, although she wore the habit of the Grey Ladies. Facilities included a clinic and a small hospital for women. Far seeing Mary helped set up medical inspection in schools in 1911 and in the same year a nurse specialising in venereal disease was appointed. The settlement ran a restaurant for nursing mothers where they could have a hot meal for 2d or 8d for 5 days paid in advance. Mothers had to stay off work for 3 months and had to bring their babies regularly to be weighed.

Her staff had to persuade mothers that care was necessary and to teach them about diet, hygiene and common sense. 'A rice biscuit dipped in whisky was believed by many young women to do a baby more good than fresh air.'

The services grew and qualified staff undertook home visits leading to Dundee's first health visitors being appointed in 1902. A girls' club with 100 members and a holiday home was opened. There was also a school for invalids which was the first special school in Dundee. On her death she bequeathed the house to provide a training school for social workers as well as its established functions. In 1918 the Social Union and the Grey Ladies Association merged. In 1912 she wrote a book entitled *Work Among Women* and also a report which is now a social history of Dundee.

Based on information in the Third Statistical Account of Scotland, Dundee 1958.

Marald Grant:

was a social worker. In 1926 she organised the Guild of Aid. Cookery classes were held for women to help them make the most of what they could afford. Clothing Exchanges were set up enabling them to cope with growing children. Creches, nurseries and holiday homes were provided through voluntary aid. She discovered that there was no adoption society for illegitimate babies so she set one up. The new 'parents' did not usually know the background of the baby but the child went to a good home.

Bonnie Fechters ~ Women in Scotland 1900-1950

MISSIONARIES

Women in the Catholic or Episcopal Church could choose to become nuns if they wished to devote their life to helping others and serving God. Presbyterians had no such outlet. The first Bachelor of Divinity in Scotland was Dr. Frances Melville in 1910 but the ministry remained a male preserve for many decades. In 1928 the Congregational Church in Scotland appointed Vera Findlay as pastor. In 1953 Mary Levison graduated as B.D. but it was 1968 before she was ordained as a Church of Scotland minister although Catherine McConnachie who graduated B.D. in 1959 was the very first woman to apply for a licence to preach after the passing of the Act of Assembly in 1956. She had served as a deaconess for 29 years. The only road open to women who wished to carry out evangelic service was to train as a doctor, nurse or teacher and become a missionary. After a period of training women missionaries were sent out by the Church, many following in the footsteps of Mary Slessor, the Dundee mill girl who became a missionary in Calabar, West Africa in 1876.

The Women's Missionary Society and its Girls Auxiliary as well as the Church of Scotland's Women's Guild Foreign Mission would raise funds in Scotland for these activities. The Catholic Women's Guild was also active in this sphere.

Island women going to a prayer meeting in the 1930's.   Third Eye Centre

PASSING THE TIME

Whether mill girl or marchioness, social life for many women took place not in visits to commercial enterprises but in organisations based in their community or church. There was very little 'public' nightlife though the cinema and dance hall did become popular.

National women's organisations had branches in Scotland run entirely by women and there were women's sections of many male organisations. The latter were usually independently run. Women also took part in mixed activities often serving on committees.

Educational classes and lectures were also open to women. Many women never did paid work or stopped earning a living when they married. Countless women spent hours helping others on a voluntary basis. It has been said that 90% of voluntary work is carried out by women.

Other women pursued hobbies or took up a sport and most women were involved in some way in fund raising through fetes, concerts, whist drives, beetle drives, dances and daffodil teas.

Reading through oral history project interviews of women born in the first decade of the 20th century it seems that while working-class women`s own mothers rarely found time to join organisations their daughters were more likely to be involved.

Jane Haining [1897-1944]:

was born on a farm in Dumfries-shire. In 1908 she won a scholarship to Dumfries Academy and lived away from home on weekdays in a girls hostel attached to the school. She proved an able academic becoming Dux of the school. At 18 she attended Glasgow Athenaeum and took a commercial course which led to employment with J.&P. Coats, threadmakers of Paisley. As a member of Queenspark West Church in Glasgow where she took part in the teaching in the Sunday School and through involvement in the Band of Hope Jane became interested in becoming a missionary and with this in mind enrolled at the College of Domestic Science in Glasgow. She went on to St. Colm's Missionary College in Edinburgh and on completion of her studies heard of a vacancy in Budapest. Having taught herself Hungarian, at the age of 35 she received her first placement at the Church of Scotland Jewish Mission Station in Budapest. She enjoyed the work and taught the girls at the school English amongst other subjects. In 1939 Jane came back to Scotland and gave talks about the persecution of Jews which was beginning to take place in Hungary. Concerned for the safety of her charges on her recall to Budapest Jane continued her work despite instructions from the Church of Scotland advising her to return home. One day in April 1944, when Hungary was controlled by the German Army under the command of Adolph Eichmann, she was charged with espionage and taken to be questioned. She wrote letters to friends from the notorious concentration camp at Auschwitz, where thousands of Jews were being exterminated. Nothing was heard of her after July 1944 until a certificate notifying her death from catarrh was issued. This has always been seen as a cover and it is believed that she was the only Scotswoman to perhaps have been exterminated in the gas chambers by the Germans. Two stained glass windows in the now Strathbungo/Queenspark Church entitled Service and Sacrifice, commemorate her work.

Bonnie Fechters ~ Women in Scotland 1900-1950

THE WOMEN'S SOCIAL SERVICE CLUBS

grew out of clubs for the unemployed in the 1930's which existed under the auspices of the Scottish Centre for Community Service. There were over 600 of these. The Citizen's Advice Bureau grew out of the old Charity Organisation Society; the Women's Citizens Association was founded in 1920 by ex-suffragists; Towns-women's Guilds served those who lived in places with over 4000 of a population, the limit for a Women's Rural Institute.

WOMEN'S GUILDS

had been in existence since the 19th century. The Church of Scotland, the Catholic Women's Guild, the Union of Catholic Mothers and Episcopal Church drew women of their faith together to pray and give service to the church. Many churches would have collapsed financially but for the efforts of the women of the congregation. Their aims were wider than fundraising for their own church, however. Through the Home Mission they helped the poor, the Foreign Mission they contributed to those working overseas; they also supported temperance work. In 1925, the Church of Scotland set up a Jewish Mission in Europe to convert disaffected Jews to Christianity.

Lectures on many topics were presented and religious plays, often based on a Bible story or the work of the missions, were a popular feature.

WOMEN'S RURAL INSTITUTE

This originally was a Canadian movement which began in Scotland in 1917. The first branch was established in East Lothian by Catherine Blair, a suffragist. The aim of the Institutes was the social and moral improvement of country life. Branches soon appeared in villages and small towns throughout Scotland and by 1919 federations of branches were set up. The Scottish Women's Rural Institute Central Committee's first president was Clayre Anstruther-Gray from Fife. She also had the honour of being the first woman to be a Justice of the Peace in Scotland.

Women living in rural areas were delighted at this opportunity to take part in an organisation which recognised the importance of their skills in country crafts and which encouraged them to learn new skills. Many WRI's became involved in running the industrial section of the local agricultural show and also were represented at the Royal Highland Show which for the early part of this century was itinerant before settling on Ingliston, Edinburgh as its permanent home.

A varied W.R.I. programme catered for all tastes including drama, handicrafts, country dancing, lectures. Inter club competitions were popular while lectures on how to conduct a meeting and on the running of exhibitions helped instil confidence among women members.

EDUCATION

in its broadest sense had a strong appeal. Many Scottish women wanted more than just classes in sewing and cookery. They wanted to know more about the world in which they lived. Lectures on topics and issues of interest became increasingly popular and new organisations emerged in response. The Electrical Association of Women and the Women's Gas Council demonstrated the use of the latest appliances; Toastmistress Clubs instructed women in the art of public speaking; Soroptomists and the Professional Women's Association drew their members from business women and members of the professions. Women were also active in the Workers Educational Association which funded classes and provided tutors for groups which then ran independently.

There were also a number of national men's organisations which had women's sections usually run independently by a committee of women. The Rotary Club had its Inner Wheel, the Round Table its Ladies Circle, the Freemasons, the Order of the Eastern Star and the British Legion had a Women's Section. Most of these were social and fund raising organisations although the Eastern Star had chapters and was presided over by a Worthy Matron and its members were referred to as 'sister'. It had initiation ceremonies and rituals.

Hobbies and crafts clubs catered for women's interests. The Embroid-

Betty Soutter (left) [1905-1991]:

lived in Chryston and was a member of the Thistle Ladies Amateur Swimming Club in Glasgow. She won the Scottish Graceful Diving Championship for Ladies seven times, the first in 1924. She was also the West of Scotland Diving Champion for 11 years, winning the competition for the first time in 1925. She was a mathematics graduate and taught at Cumbernauld Village School. She became principal of the science department. She was a leader in Chryston Girl Guide Company. She received a commendation for rescuing a man from drowning but was herself injured in a diving accident.

Bonnie Fechters ~ Women in Scotland 1900-1950

1. 35th Glasgow Boy Scouts. 2. YWCA. 3. Chryston Girl Guides. 4. 1st Twechar Girls Guildry ~ Twechar Parish Church of Scotland.

erers Guild, horticultural societies, art classes and many other opportunities in this field were provided through Local Authority Continuing Education and Community Centres. The Women's League of Health and Beauty was popular with those who enjoyed aesthetic exercise and there were also keep-fit groups.

YOUTH WORK

gave women a chance to serve the boys and girls of their community. Sunday school teaching, Guilds of Friendship and girls' clubs needed leaders. The uniformed organisations such as the Girl Guides, Girls Guildry, Boy's Brigade and the cub section of the Boy Scouts needed young women who would willingly give a lot of their time voluntarily to run the meetings and camps. As well as running clubs, the Young Women's Christian Association ran hostels for girls working away from home.

Enjoying yourself might seem like hard work. Nevertheless all these organisations helped women to learn about responsibility, loyalty and the qualities needed for committee work to run them successfully.

The more worrying aspect was that the members of these organisations were mainly drawn from the middle-class and skilled working-class. Many of these women gave a lifetime of devoted service and set a good example to young people.

Before the creation of the National Assistance Board and the National Health Service, the importance of charity and voluntary work indicates that there must have been a vast number of women and girls living in poverty and in need of help. The funds raised by all this voluntary effort came from the pockets of local people but required a great deal of work and commitment. Paying for services out of taxation would not perhaps have been as much fun. In the days before television changed social life for ever, having an excuse to get out of the house for an evening was probably welcomed with open arms.

There are countless women whose lives touched others and whose stories are rarely recorded. Volumes could be written about their struggles, ingenuity and ability to see the funny side of life. These bonnie fechters who were willing to depart from the image of the 'angel of the house' enriched their own lives through involvement. At the same time they helped other women to gain confidence and a belief in their own abilities. This ultimately resulted in wider opportunities for women in the second half of the 20th century. *The End*

Bonnie Fechters ~ Women in Scotland 1900-1950

ACKNOWLEDGEMENTS

Thanks are due to local history librarians throughout Scotland for their help and permission to reproduce photographs and other material. I would especially like to thank:

Alan Reid, SLA Publications Officer

Brian Osborne, Chief officer, Libraries & Museums, Strathkelvin District Libraries

Ian Copland, District Librarian, North East Fife District Libraries

Ken Willox,

Ruth Currie,

Ian MacDougall,

Rev. Norma Stewart,

Maria Fyfe M.P.,

Gordon Baxter, Chairman, Baxter's of Speyside

Janetta Bowie,

Sandie Shaw,

Pat Malcolm, Clydebank District Libraries

Don Martin, Strathkelvin District Libraries

Marion McLean,

Elizabeth Dunlop,

Valerie Boa, McLean Museum, Greenock

Audrey Canning, STUC Library

Dalmuir Education Resource Centre,

Central Region School Library Service,

Staff of Strathkelvin District Libraries,

E. Smith, W.R.V.S. Information Officer.

Katy Gardiner

Thanks are also due to David Winter, Dundee, for permission to quote from Sidlaw Breezes by Mary Brooksbank.

Scott Ballantyne, Designer.

TEACHERS NOTES

With **Bonnie Fechters**, Sheila Livingstone has provided an invaluable book for teachers and pupils within the Secondary School. This collection of wide ranging accounts, memories and photographs describing the lives of Scottish women during the first half of this century is a unique resource. During a period of great social and political change throughout Europe, this book gives an insight into the part women in Scotland played - a part often unrecognized in a male dominated society. From the well educated upper class women's involvement in the struggle for women's vote to the working class women in grass roots politics and to the sheer hard work of the thousands of women who kept the factories going in war time and the families together at all times, it is all here.

This book is of particular use at the middle and upper end of the Secondary School -

1. STANDARD GRADE

Bonnie Fechters provides excellent source and support material for:

• Unit 1 - Changing life in Scotland and Britain, both Contexts B (1830s - 1930s) and C (1880s - present day)

• Unit 2 - International Cooperation and Conflict, Contexts B & C especially the effects on people's lives at the Home Front.

• The Investigation. This is not only a resource for investigating women's history but other aspects of social and political history.

2. REVISED HIGHER Option 1850s - 1970s. Again **Bonnie Fechters** is a valuable resource.

While of specific relevance to prescribed syllabi, **Bonnie Fechters** has a much wider and more general use to teachers in supporting Equal Opportunities policies. This book not only catalogues individual women's lives, its ethos is an encouragement to all women, pupil or teacher, to take a full role in contemporary society. No History Department should be without a copy.

Ruth Currie, a history teacher, was a full-time member of the Curriculum Development team in Dumbarton Division, Strathclyde. She now teaches Modern Studies at Chryston High School.

Money conversion table:		
1/-	=	5p
2/-	=	10p
5/-	=	25p
10/-	=	50p
30/-	=	£1.50p

FURTHER READING

Well researched novels can give an insight into everyday life during this period. The following authors are recommended.

George Blake, Margaret Thomson Davis, Lewis Grassic Gibbon, Robin Jenkins, Jessie Kesson, William McIlvanney, Frederick Niven, Jan Webster.

Factual:

Bowie, Janetta~ *Penny Buff*, Constable, 1975.
" " *Penny Boss* " 1976.
" " *Penny Change* " 1977.
Memories of school teaching in the West of Scotland.

Breitenbach, E. and Gordon, E. ~ *Out of Bounds: Women in Scottish Society 1800-1945*, Edinburgh University Press, 1993.

Cope, Zachary ~ *Six Disciples of Florence Nightingale*, Pitman 1961.

Damer, Sean ~ *Rent Strike*, Glasgow Labour, 1982.

Gordon, Eleanor ~ *Women's Sphere in People and Society in Scotland*, v.2., p229

King, Elspeth ~ *Hidden from History, the Thenew Factor*, Mainstream 1993

Leneman, Leah ~ *A Guid Cause; the Women's Suffrage Movement in Scotland*, Aberdeen University Press,1991.

Long, Elliot ~ *St. Mungo's Bairns.*

MacDougall, Ian ed. *Hard Work Ye Ken, Four Midlothian Women Farmworkers*, Canongate 1993.

Stevenson, Joyce ed. ~ *Five Bob a Week-Stirling Women's Work 1900-1950*, Stirling District Council, 1988.

Young, James ~ *Women and Popular Struggles*, Mainstream, 1985.

Scottish Women and the Vote; a Collection of Source Material on the Campaign for Women's Suffrage in Scotland, Strathclyde Regional Council, 1993

(Mainly Women's Social & Political Union)

T.V. programmes and videos:

Time Quines, Scottish Television.

Time Gentlemen Please, BBC.

Scottish Women's Hospital Unit, Scottish Film Archive.

Change in the 20th century, Scottish Film Archive.

Bonnie Fechters ~ Women in Scotland 1900-1950

A

Aberdeen, Countess of 7, 18
abstainers 4, 41, 42
accountants 12, 38
adoption 42
advertisements 7, 22, 23, 35
agencies, domestic 7
Air Raid Precautions 33, 34
air taxi 14,15
air transport auxiliary 29
anaesthetics 36
Anglo - Yugoslav Children's Hospital 30
Anti - Conscription League 25
Anti - Suffrage League 21
Anti - Sweating League 22
Anti - War Movement 8, 22, 25
apprenticeship 28
Armistice 8, 33
artificial limbs 27
asylums 38
Auxiliary Territorial Service 29

B

bailie 19, 22
Band of Hope 42
birth control 37
blitz 33
Blood Transfusion Service 40
British Women's Temperance Association 37, 41, 42
Brooksbank, Mary 8, 22
Burnbank Missionary Training House 41

C

Cat and Mouse Act 18
catering 11, 28, 34
Catholic League of the Cross 42
Catholic Women's Guild 32, 43
Catholic Women's Suffrage Society 18
charities 20, 35, 37, 38, 41
Charity Organisation Society 37, 44
charity work 19, 20, 37, 41
child welfare 19, 30, 37
childbirth 35, 36, 37
Childrens Clothing Guild 37
choirs 10
Church of Scotland 21, 37, 43, 44
Civil Service 11, 15
Clothing Exchange 34, 42
clothing societies 37, 42
Clyde Commission for the Dilution of Labour 27
Clyde Workers Committee 27
Coalmining 9, 14, 15
Communism 8, 9, 25, 33, 37
Conciliation Bill 1912 18
conductresses 29, 32
confectionery trade 6, 9, 10
Congregational Church 40
conscientious objectors 30
conscription 26
convalescent homes 38, 41
cooks 7, 8, 11, 30
Co-operative Movement 22, 43
county councillors 18, 20, 22
Cranston, Kate 11, 41
creches 16, 17, 37, 42
'crying' meetings 17, 22

D

dancing 10, 12, 15, 42
dangerous substances 27
Dilution 16, 26, 27
Disabled Soldiers and Sailors Fund 32
District Nursing Associations 21, 37, 41
divorce 16
doctors 6, 18, 26, 30, 31, 32, 34, 35, 36, 38-39, 40
domestic service 5, 6, 7, 8, 9, 13, 21, 28, 41
Dorcas Societies 37
dressmakers 15, 23
driving 26, 29, 33
Duke Street Prison 18

E

Earl Haig Fund 20
Eastern Star, Order of the 44
'egg' money 13
Electrical Association of Women 44
Elsie Inglis Maternity Hospital 38
Entertainers National Service Association 28
equal pay 23, 24
evacuation 21, 26, 34

F

factories 5, 6, 8, 9, 14, 22, 23, 26
factors 13, 16, 24
Factory Acts 6, 10
family allowances 21, 26
farmwork 6, 9, 13, 26
First Aid Nursing Yeomanry 30
fish gutters 14
fishing 6, 10, 14, 23
fishing net workers 9, 23
fishwives 10, 14
Flying Nursing Orderlies 29
foreign missions 43
Friendly Societies 32, 38
fresh air fortnights 37, 41

G

General Assembly of the Church of Scotland 21
Girl Guides 19, 37, 44, 45
Girls Auxiliary of the Women's Missionary Society 43
girls' clubs 19, 42, 45
Girls Guildry 45
Glasgow & West of Scotland Association for Women's Suffrage 18, 23
Glasgow Council for Women's Trades 23
Glasgow Nurses Club 40
Green Ladies 29, 32
Grey Ladies 42
Guild of Aid 42

H

health visitors 29, 32, 37, 42
herbwives 35, 36
Hoggie's Angels 13
holiday homes 41
hospitals 8, 18, 30, 31, 32, 33, 35, 36, 37, 38, 41
hostels 7, 8
hotels 11, 26, 33
howdies 35, 36, 37
hunger marches 16, 25
hunger strikes 18
hydropathics 36
Hyslop, Janet 24, 33

I

Independent Labour Party 18, 22, 25
industrial action 15, 22-24
industrial schools 7, 8, 19
Inglis, Elsie 31, 32, 38
International Brigade 9, 33
International Council of Nurses 40
Irwin, Margaret 11, 23

J

Jewish Mission 43

K

L

labour exchange 21, 27
Ladies Auxiliary 40
lady's maid 7
laundresses 8
Little White Ribboners 42
local government 11, 18, 19

M

maids 7
Means Test 25
Medical Women's Federation 38
medicines 35, 36
Members of Parliament 17, 20-21
midwifery 36, 39
midwives 36
Midwives Act 1915 36, 37
Military nursing services 19, 30, 33
mills 6, 8, 9, 23, 26
ministers of religion 43
missionaries 6, 40, 41, 43
missions 19, 36, 41, 42
Moral Rearmament Society 25
Muirhead Trust 25
munitions 4, 8, 26, 27
Murray, Eunice 17, 18, 28

Bonnie Fechters ~ Women in Scotland 1900-1950

INDEX

N

nannies	6, 7
National Council of Women	19
National Egg Collection for Wounded Soldiers	32
National Farmers Union	21
National Federation of Women Workers	11, 22, 23
National Female Franchise Association	18
National Health Act 1948	37, 41
National Insurance Act 1911	35
National Trust	17
National Union of Mineworkers	25
National Vigilance Committee	7, 41
No-Conscription Fellowship	25
Northern Men's Federation for Women's Suffrage	17
nurseries	33, 34, 37, 42
nurses	23, 26-28, 30-33, 36, 39-41
nursing	6, 29, 30, 31, 33, 39-41

O

office work	9, 11, 24, 25, 26
Onward and Upward Association	7
orphans	7, 8, 11, 41
outings	10

P

Pankhursts, The	18
Parliamentary candidates	17, 18, 20, 21, 22, 23
Patriotic Work Parties	19, 32
peace movement	16, 25
philanthropists	39, 41
police work	14, 15, 19
Princess Mary's R.A.F. Nursing Service	29
prisoners of war	19, 31, 32
professional organisations	44
professors	38, 39
provosts	19, 20
puerpal fever	37

Q

Queen Alexandra's Nursing Service	30
Queen Mary's Army Auxiliary Corps	29

R

radium	39
railways	9, 26, 27, 28, 38
Red Cross Societies	19, 20, 21, 26, 30, 31, 33
'Red' Duchess	21
rent strikes	16, 24
Representation of the People Act, 1918	20
restaurants	11, 34, 37, 41
retailing	6, 9, 10, 11, 12, 13, 22, 24
Right to Work Bill	28
Royal Commission on Women's Working Conditions	6, 23

S

Salvation Army	41, 43
Save the Children Fund	30
scientists	5
Scotswoman of the Year, 1970	21
Scottish Association of Manufacturers Agents	12, 13
Scottish Co-operative Women's Guild	18, 25, 32, 37
Scottish Council for Nuclear Disarmament	25
Scottish Council for Women's Trades	11
Scottish Federation of Women's Suffrage Societies	18, 31, 38
Scottish Housewives Association	25
Scottish Trades Union Congress	22, 23, 24, 25
Scottish Women's Suffrage Society	18
Scottish Women's Ambulance Unit	30
Scottish Women's Conference of the T.U.C.	21
Scottish Women's Hospital Unit	30, 31, 32, 39
searchlight regiments	29
Sex Disqualification [Removal] Act 1919	15, 28
shipyards	27, 26
shop assistants	9, 10, 11, 19, 22, 26
Shop Assistants Union	22
shrouds	36
singing	9, 10, 42
social unions	42
social workers	16, 29, 41, 42
Soldiers and Sailors Families Association	32
Soroptomists	44
Spanish Civil War	9, 21, 33
sport	10, 42, 44
Stepps Equal Rights Society	24
stokers	26
street sweepers	15
strikes	9, 11, 23-24
substitution	28
suffrage societies	16, 17-19
suffragists	17-19, 21, 22, 23, 38, 44

T

Tax Resistance League	18
teachers	6, 9, 11, 15, 29, 40, 44
Temperance Movement	11, 16, 22, 36, 40, 41, 42
Territorial Nursing Force	29, 30
Toastmistresses	44
tonic wine	35, 36
trade unions	9, 10, 11, 16, 22, 25, 27, 28, 38
truck system	22, 23

U

United Nations Organisation	21, 30

V

venereal disease	37, 42
Victoria, Queen	4
Voluntary Aid Detachments	19, 21, 30, 31, 41
Voluntary Hospitals	37
volunteers	16, 26, 34, 41

W

waitresses	6, 11, 23
War Emergency Workers National Committee	23
washerwomen	6, 8
weavers	6, 8, 9, 43
welders	26
white leg	37
widows	6, 28, 39
Wings for Victory Weeks	18
Women for Westminster	25
Women's Army Auxiliary Corps	29
Women's Auxiliary Air Force	29
Women's Burns Club	20
Women's Citizens Association	44
Women's County Committee of the Women's Land Army	30
Women's Freedom League	17, 38
Women's Gas Council	44
women's guilds	8, 9, 32, 43, 44
Women's Labour League	25
Women's Land Army	21, 30
Women's League of Health & Beauty	45
Women's Legion	25, 29, 43
Women's Liberal Association	18, 19, 21
Women's Missionary Society	43
Women's Parliament	34
Women's Protective and Provident League	23
Women's Royal Airforce	29
Women's Royal Naval Service	28, 29
Women's Royal Voluntary Service	34
Women's Rural Institute	18, 44
Women's Services	28-40
Women's Social and Political Union	17, 38
Women's Social Service Clubs	44
Women's Suffrage National Aid Corps	18
Women's Timber Corps	30
Women's Trade Union League	22
Women's Unionist Association	19, 20, 21
Women's University Settlement	41
Women's Voluntary Service	20, 34
Workers Educational Association	44
Working Women's Guild	8

X

Y

Young Communist League	25
Young Unionist Association	20
Young Women's Christian Association	41, 45

Z

Zenana Societies	37

Bonnie Fechters ~ Women in Scotland 1900-1950